TELL THE TRUTH,

SHAME THE DEVIL

Smyth & Helwys Publishing, Inc.
6316 Peake Road
Macon, Georgia 31210-3960
1-800-747-3016
©2015 by James Ellis III, ed.
All rights reserved.

Library of Congress Cataloging-in-Publication Data

Tell the truth, shame the devil : stories about the challenges of young pastors / James Ellis III, editor.
pages cm
ISBN 978-1-57312-839-1 (pbk. : alk. paper)
1. Pastoral theology. I. Ellis, James, III, editor.
BV4015. T45 2015
253--dc23

2015031304

Tell the Truth, Shame the Devil

Stories about the Challenges of Young Pastors

JAMES ELLIS III, ED.

Also by James Ellis III

OnThaGrindCuzin: The School Daze of Being "Incognegro" in 1619

Dedication

Dedicated to Jesus, who "is, and was, and is to come" (Rev 1:1),
and to those who wrestle with their call to vocational ministry.
If nothing else, this publication is a beautiful illustration that
"faith is the assurance of things hoped for,
the conviction of things not seen" (Heb 11:1).
God is our strength and refuge.

Contents

Clergy > 35

Foreword

Elizabeth Roebke Sillerud

I knew I loved the man who would become my husband when, after dating for just three months, the holy day of Good Friday approached. My then-boyfriend knew that what is a regular day for some was for me a day of high job-performance stress coupled with real spiritual weight. He works in sales of industrial parts, so this was new territory for him.

How do I support my pastor girlfriend upon the death of the Savior?

I knew I loved him when, after our evening worship service, he met me at the door with flowers, chocolates, and the invitation to watch mindless television. He understood me—as pastor and girlfriend. I knew then that he was a gift from God meant just for me.

Clergy can be hard cards to read. It is easy to assume that with the help of God, we've got it all together. Our houses are always tidy, our laundry is always folded, we never forget to send cards on our mother's birthdays, and we always have a sandwich in our back pocket to give to a person in need. The projection is that to be a leader in the church, to be a prophet among God's people, to be a shepherd of the sheep, clergy ought to have all their ducks in a row.

Well, this October, my now-husband and I forgot my mother-in-law's birthday. It came amid the early months of our daughter's life, the annual confirmation retreat, an approaching Reformation Sunday celebration, and my attempt at balancing being a mom and pastor for the first time—which amounts to two of the world's least predictable schedules colliding. My mother-in-law showed us grace. She let it go, acknowledging that we were rightfully distracted by the smiles on our little girl's face. But I'd hate to ask, what if her pastor forgot? What if her pastor failed to mail a card on a significant occasion? Would this person receive such mercy? Could such a simple slip lead to dividing issues in a church?

The following collection of essays speaks to both sides of this relationship. It names the real struggles of clergy under age thirty-five who are piecing together a pastoral identity in a church that the world fears is dying. It also names the evils that congregations and denominations can knowingly and often unknowingly inflict upon their pastors. While the call to ministry is life giving, joyful, and Spirit led, our sinful selves and the presence of sin in others cannot be ignored. It is vital to hear from other young clergy that you are not alone. It is insightful to share with laypeople the peculiar realities of life in ministry that they cannot imagine (i.e., remember to pump the septic tank before the annual church supper!). It is a hopeful act to tell the truth and shame the devil so that we, clergy and laypeople alike, might support a new generation of imperfect ministers who are called to share with us the love of God.

If one of the things everyone assumes about clergy is that we are in constant prayer, that we are perfect in our personal devotional lives while also tending to the spiritual (and other) needs of "our people," then hear this collection of essays as prayers. Some are prayers of lament, some of joy, some of grief, some of hope, some of exasperation, some of praise. Each essay is a prayer for the future of the church and for its young leaders. Each essay longs to end with an "amen" asking God into its story. Take care of this gift you have been given, a window into the lives of young clergy, and pray for them and for the church. Hear their pain, hear their joy, hear their truth. The truth will set you free, said the Savior who died on Good Friday, and then he rose again so that we might all know of his love.

ELIZABETH ROEBKE SILLERUD is a native Minnesotan serving as an Associate Pastor at American Lutheran Church in Billings, Montana. An ordained Lutheran, she holds the MDiv from Yale Divinity School with a Certificate of Advanced Theological Studies from Pacific Lutheran Seminary, and BA in Art History from Boston College.

Acknowledgments

For a sometimes lonely, introverted vagabond like me, God has been not only my redeeming refuge through life's storms but also my very best friend. I have been bestowed talents and permitted experiences that aren't easy to manage and that at times conflict with the calculations of my flesh, but that I yet know are intended to strengthen me. God is good, and no individual or circumstance can convince me otherwise. Call that naïveté if you like. I promise I won't get bent out of shape about it. I have experienced much worse, none of which is comparable to the wonderment I feel at God's love and power.

Long before this book was conceptualized, my wife was my biggest fan, reassuring my labor as a young writer and pastor, and encouraging me to follow my dreams. In her I find a kindred devotee of Jesus. I am thankful that we are both committed to the church but also that we both refuse to sugarcoat, spiritualize, or dismiss glitches of how our communities often worship the Lord and approach ministry. Marriage is hard enough on its own, and marriage to a husband whose vocation requires shepherding ornery two-legged sheep can easily be too much to bear. So, to my wife, Renata, thank you for your love, devotion, and growth. As I have said through the years, our union as husband and wife will always be the most important ministry to me.

Most of us don't traverse life by sheer will; rather, we receive help from someone somehow at one point or another. I am indebted to Dr. James E. Massey, Dr. M. Craig Barnes, and Dr. Eugene H. Peterson for their advocacy and conversation. Their witness is the kindling that inspires me to be my authentic self in Christ. As they have for me many times over, I hope to create new access points and opportunities for young pastors to gain their professional footing and find their theological voices. Towards that end, George W. Truett Theological Seminary at Baylor University and Pittsburgh Theological Seminary are sacred spaces to me. It was in matriculating at both institutions that I began engaging in theological inquiry, which resulted in experiences that have been truly formative.

As a Guthrie Scholar, in September of 2013 I spent a brief time in residence at Columbia Theological Seminary. Collaborating with Dr. Israel Galindo, the late Dr. Stephen A. Hayner, Dr. Paul Johnson, Dr. Kimberly B. Long, and Dr. Sarah F. Erickson was like meeting old friends for the first time. Through the online blogosphere, Rev. Peter Wallace at *Day1* has graciously given me a platform to share my writings with a broad audience, which has been a godsend. And to the pastors who have found occasion to open their pulpits to me and lend support in other ways, I offer thanks. Respectively, Rev. Elizabeth Roebke Sillerud and Dr. Eldon Fry have penned a lovely opening and closing to this collection, as I knew they would. I hold them both in high esteem.

Having known her since my undergraduate days at the University of Maryland, I feel that Dr. Judith H. Paterson is, in a phrase, class personified. I am happy to call her friend and mentor. She is a literary muse whose cheerleading, hospitality, and sincerity warm my soul. Having officiated my wedding and ordination, Rev. Andy Davis has a special place in my heart. I hope that I make him and the good people of the First Baptist Church of Belton proud. Dr. John Erwin, Jean Young, Margaret Harper, and Eugene Pearson have all been so kind to me. I deeply appreciate your help in keeping me buoyed to God through all manner of inclement weather.

Not to be forgotten, this book is impossible without its contributors. I commend their bravery and thank Smyth & Helwys for their validation. I pray that our stories inspire others to "run with perseverance" the marathon of life, a unique journey that for those in the pastoral vocation carries personal and professional implications, since our faith and vocation intersect at so many points. Thank you for telling the truth. To the people I have served and co-labored with in this sojourn of ministry, in Jesus' name I offer my warmest regards. To God's faithful near and far, keep the faith even as Jesus Christ, the author and finisher of our faith, keeps us.

James Ellis III
Waldorf, Maryland

Introduction

The seeds for this book were planted during my early years of ministry and graduate theological study. In bookstores and libraries I found an abundance of resources on preaching effectively, organizing successful stewardship campaigns, launching small groups, and planting churches, but few that substantively addressed the pastoral vocation as a whole or even dared to critique it with language that people aside from academicians readily understood. While helpful, the few pastoral theology/leadership books I did come across that spoke to this were usually authored by older pastors at the twilight of their career, or those otherwise far removed from the often erratic catacombs of ministry. The decades of insight that seasoned clergy have amassed is priceless. But still, the somewhat exclusive telling of their stories quickly revealed an enormous generational gulf with young pastors like me who are trying to make "holy sense" of our call. It began to seem that young pastors were merely an afterthought, valued conceptually but not where the rubber meets the road. Being selected as a 2012–2013 Lewis Fellow at Wesley Theological Seminary—a post-graduate, post-ordination leadership development program for clergy under thirty-five—was a great help in further piecing the puzzle together. I quickly learned that young pastors are desperate for candid resources they can relate to, composed by and for their peers. Additionally, we need books that represent more than the experiences of white, male clergy and ministry scholars reflective of just one denominational hue. This project was birthed through a profound yearning to speak to this need.

Tell the Truth, Shame the Devil: Stories about the Challenges of Young Pastors is a collection of real-life stories written primarily by pastoral leaders thirty-five years old or younger, wherein they reflect on challenging experiences of their journey in ministry. Taking a page from the black Christian vernacular, "telling the truth and shaming the devil" is an affirmation that truth is our best policy to bless and be blessed. Speaking the truth in love (Eph 4:15) undergirds this concept alongside the belief that "to obey is better than sacrifice" (1 Sam 15:22). Pastors inevitably experience bumps, bruises, and even suffering as servant leaders, sometimes "in the name of God." Shepherding God's sheep is a joyous privilege, yet it is not without heartache, injustice, and profane tension. The aim of this book, then, is to highlight that unfortunate paradox, hoping that young pastors will no longer face their veiled struggles alone.

You will be hard pressed to find cookie-cutter platitudes here. These accounts are from the crypt of secrecy and often go unaddressed, usually shared only between a few colleagues or close friends. In exposing vocational struggles, evil can be robbed of its power to cast shame, depression, and isolation on future pastors who will guide Christianity in an ever-changing mission field. In an effort to foster intergenerational dialogue, the book ends with stories from pastoral leaders over the age of thirty-five. This was a critical component to include because these faithful servants, too, have endured many trials through their careers and likewise deserve a safe space to share.

With backgrounds and places of service that vary greatly, from higher education, the local church, and beyond, the contributors represent an impressive degree of diversity. I am grateful for their willingness to bare their souls. Both genders are well represented, along with a cornucopia of theological traditions: Episcopal, Baptist, United Methodist, Assemblies of God, Lutheran, United Church of Christ, Church of the Brethren, Christian Church (Disciples of Christ), and Foursquare. As aggressive as I was in trying to procure even more representation of biblical Christianity's rich theological kaleidoscope, it simply didn't work out as fully as I would have liked. Some denominations and clergy lacked the time or interest to be involved, which I understand. Even so, what has been assembled, as it is still so diverse, has the capacity to touch a wide range of people, allowing it to make a noteworthy impact as a candid introduction to the ever-fluid challenges of vocational ministry.

I hope this will be a transformative resource for all pastors, but principally for young clergy, for those who may be discerning a call to ministry, and also for those generally interested in the behind-the-scenes ecclesiology of "church life." The most important value that undergirds this book is forthrightness. There is no doubt that the impending level of transparency is risky, rendering its authors vulnerable. In ways and means unique to our experience, each contributor's objective is to "tell the truth, the whole truth, and nothing but the truth." Eugene H. Peterson's sobering scholarship has served as a significant source of inspiration as this book has developed. His words speak volumes, particularly in *The Jesus Way: A Conversation on the Ways that Jesus Is the Way*:

> Being religious does not translate across the board into being good or trustworthy. Religion is one of the best covers for sin of almost all kinds. Pride, anger, lust, and greed are vermin that flourish under the floorboards of religion. Those of us who are identified with institutions or vocations in religion can't be too vigilant. The devil does some of his best work behind stained glass.[1]

Elaborating on the toll of vocational ministry as young pastors can place a heavy burden on the mind, body, and soul. I am eternally grateful to all contributors for investing in the truth in such a constructive way.

A central hope for *Tell the Truth, Shame the Devil* is that those outside Christianity will also be enlightened to read of experiences that pastors of all stripes suffer through: the at times hellish circumstances that are perhaps unknown to the public. Being a leader of any kind anywhere is tough, but shepherding God's sheep may just take the cake. The conflicts, dishonesty, mistreatment, racism, sexism, ageism, and theological harassment and exclusion render the context of church work quite unique in its challenges. In another way, by inviting the larger pastoral world (parishioners, lay leaders, denominational staff, those in higher education, etc.) into these conversations, young pastors will be encouraged to know that they are not alone in struggling with the demands of their calling—the unimagined, collateral carnage that they encounter. With God and those bold enough to be faithful to the countercultural ethics of the Bible, hope, healing, and help are available even for—especially for—our caretakers of "the faith."

Christian faith is not a path of ease or least resistance, and mixing the sensitive elements of vocational ministry, graduate education, family, and other experiences can at times explode like a Molotov cocktail on one's soul. Contrary to the caricatures, life as a young pastor is not all about hymns, incense, prayer, pageantry, and monastic reflection. For most of us, it is or can be an extremely rocky road full of bewilderment and mystery, no matter how much love we have for the people we serve and the work we are called to do. Therefore, Paul's words to the church at Philippi ages ago speak strongly to us still today: we know that the good work the Lord has begun in us will accomplish its purpose (Phil 1:6). May these stories communicate God's power, peace, and presence to all who read them.

Clergy ≤ 35

Of Spirit and Mind: A Pentecostal's Battle Against Depression

Ryan Beaty

There was a chill in the night air, so we chose to sit indoors. We were at one of my city's most well-liked pizza parlors in the hip, regentrified part of town. We had gone on dates for about two months and she obviously knew I was a pastor, which was a breath of fresh air since most women I encountered ran like Usain Bolt upon learning of my calling. She liked to talk, often much more than I, about my job, so when she brought up the subject of ministry while we ate, I was not surprised.

"So ministry is hard, right?" she commented more than questioned. "How do you deal with the difficulty?"

Thinking nothing of the question I responded, "Yeah, ministry is hard. But I have really good friends I talk to all the time who are also in ministry. We share each other's burdens. I have other non-ministry friends whom I can just *be me* with. And I see a counselor every Thursday morning. Talking to him is the best thing I do for myself as well as the church. He also has me taking a low-dose serotonin booster, which is an anti-depressant."

She stopped eating and looked at me. "Are you serious?" Again, she was more commenting than questioning. "Why would you go see a counselor? They don't have any wisdom. They can't help you. Are you depressed?"

"Yes," I said, "I have dealt with depression and do battle with it occasionally. My counselor helps me."

"But depression is a spirit," she retorted. "Why not just pray and praise it away?"

"If you mean a spirit as in a disposition, then okay, I can see that. But if you mean a spirit as in a demon then no, you are wrong. Depression isn't a demon."

"Sure it is," she said.

"No it isn't," I replied.

"Yes it is!" she said.

The conversation carried on for a few minutes at a high level of intensity, culminating with her insinuation that if I was "more saved" and had "more faith," then I wouldn't struggle with depression. For some reason, she and I never went out again.

This was not, however, the first time I have encountered such attitudes from people within my faith tradition and broader Christianity. I grew up in and am ordained in a classical Pentecostal denomination. For many within it, the idea of depression and mental illness has been completely associated with the influence of the spirit realm. We learned phrases like, "Demons can oppress your body, depress your mind, and possess your soul if you let them." And if some physical maladies are at times caused by evil spirits, as several New Testament authors lead us to believe, many people in turn believe that most if not all mental issues are the direct result of demonic activity. I happen to be of a vein of Christianity that still believes in a literal Satan and demonic spirits, but I don't believe that they are the cause of all our problems. For the source of the vast majority of our issues, we need look no further than the mirror.

I began dealing with depression at an early age, though undiagnosed. I have always been a big kid. Weight has been a constant issue for me, and like most kids who are different, my self-image was affected by how others related to me as a result of my difference. I didn't think I was as valuable or as important as other kids. I couldn't imagine a scenario where a girl would want to date me, so I seldom made an effort. I carried those feelings and images of myself into adulthood.

I also sensed a call to ministry from an early age. I always knew this was my future and have never really considered doing anything else. When you are the kid who is sensing this leading for your life, you *do* act differently than other children. You try to be a good example and to do the right thing. Kids start noticing this, and it causes you to assume a pastoral role in their lives and carry responsibilities that you are not prepared for. You start to feel pressured to be a spiritual person in ways that you are not yet able, and the adults around you see it too. So they begin to lift you up as an example and give you more responsibility. Have you ever wondered what type of mental weight a kid like this could be carrying? How about the fact that the fat kid feels the pressure of his entire school going to hell if he doesn't set a good example? Oh, and he needs to get good grades and get into college too.

That kind of pressure doesn't go away when you enter ministry. It intensifies. Most of us have been carrying the weight of others' spiritual conditions for much longer than we have truly been clergy. For all practical purposes, we were clergy before we ever graduated seminary, received our stole, or donned that white collar. We assumed a role in people's lives before our denominations ever approved us to do so. And when we stepped into the pulpit for the first time, it began hitting us like a ton of bricks.

Herein lies the problem. As a result of our responsibilities—sermon preparation, hospital visits, leadership development, pastoral counseling, committee forming, etc.—we take on a role that was never ours. In many ways, we become God for some of our parishioners. Our job is supposed to help guide people to God, but instead we sometimes become God for them. The bricks started becoming too much for me in November 2011. A little over a year earlier, I left my dream job at my denomination's headquarters to answer a call to my birth city to plant a church among urban people adjacent to one of America's top-fifteen universities. I not only left my dream job but also said goodbye to the town where I went to seminary. It had become home. I left steady income. I left a support network of friends. I left a church that I enjoyed. And I moved to a place to do ministry with people whom no one else seemed to want.

To get ready, I went to church-plant bootcamps, read books, and started developing a launch team. I raised tens of thousands of dollars. At the same time I began to heap expectations upon myself. I was going to do what no one else had ever done. I was going to raise a godly church among people whose gods had been education and success. I was going to be an example for my denomination and a pattern for others to follow. I was going to single-handedly, with the Holy Spirit's assistance of course, affect the spiritual climate of my city. I could do it all.

I was two months into the life of my new church when I returned to my former hometown to take part in a wedding. I was only there for seventy-two hours, but I came back from that trip discouraged. All but two members of my launch team were gone. We had no money. My new church was averaging a whopping seven people. And for seventy-two hours I was confronted with everything great that I had left behind. I was nowhere near where I expected or planned to be with the new church plant.

The space between expectation and reality is called frustration. Now my frustration got to hang out with what I had sacrificed, and the two had a baby named *depression*. My life, my church, my ministry wasn't what I wanted it to be. I was a failure. I had heard of churches that launched their first Sunday with hundreds of people. We had thirty-seven on our first day. Thirty-one of them were friends and family who came to wish us well. I figured it was my fault. People weren't putting their trust in Christ because of something I was doing wrong. We weren't growing because of something I wasn't doing right. I wasn't praying or fasting enough. I needed to do more! It was all about me.

That's a load we were never meant to carry. It can drive us to the bottle, the psych ward, or the grave. Thankfully, it drove me to a Christian counselor. I chose my counselor because my insurance would pay for him and because the clinic where he worked was about thirty minutes from the church I lead. I didn't want to encounter any of the people from church when I went to sessions. I didn't want them to know their pastor had problems. As far as they were concerned, all they needed to know was that I had it all together. I was their spiritual rock. Their eternal destiny hung in the balance of my hands. If they found out I went to a counselor, they would doubt Christ, become apostate, commit blasphemy, and *burn baby burn*!

So put yourself in my shoes. I hate myself because I suck at life: thirty-two years old, single, still chubby, and broke. I suck at ministry; my church is still small, finances are tight, and I'm bi-vocational, so I can't devote all the time I want to the entire reason I moved here. I have been forced to get mental help and start antidepressants, so I feel like a weak and pathetic loser! I hit rock bottom, and that's when God went to work.

When I first met Mark, I didn't like him—not because of anything he said or did but because he physically resembled a guy I had had an issue with several years ago. I thought there was no way I could receive help from a guy whom I kind of wanted to punch in the face. That of course was another example of me being a miserable failure as a pastor, because pastors don't punch people. It's like the eleventh commandment or something. As we began to talk, however, things changed. I learned that Mark spent decades in the pulpit before becoming a therapist. He had also participated in a variety of denominational offerings that set him on course for stardom within his church. Then it all came crashing down, and he found himself in therapy and on antidepressants. I was so relieved to hear I wasn't the only one. We started meeting weekly.

That is when God went to work through my counselor. Mark began relating to me in ways I didn't think anyone else could. He understood what I was saying about my frustrations and suggested Scriptures that helped me understand that a number of Bible heroes such as Elijah and Paul went through similar seasons when they dealt with depression. He began talking to me about the role I was assuming in people's lives. I am not God. I shouldn't try to be. I am not the rock in which people put their faith. I am not the answer to their problems. I am not their protector. I am a companion on their faith journey. Even my own burdens don't belong to me. Christ said to cast my cares on him. I also started a regiment of antidepressants. That was its own moral dilemma. Being Pentecostal, we believe in divine healing. Why couldn't I have enough faith for God to heal me? If my brain is sick, then God needs to fix it! But I called a mentor and talked to him about what was going on, and his response was short and to the point: "Take the drugs!" God also went to work through the drugs. I feel much better when I take them. My low moments are not anywhere close to being as low. At one point I spent a week in bed not because I was sick but because I was sick of what was out there. I don't have those days anymore. It's not solely because of the antidepressants, but I know they help.

God continued to work through my circumstances, and I began to appreciate how much I like the job I do to pay the bills. I also began to appreciate the great things that are happening in my church. We have accomplished huge dreams. The very fact that we are still around is a testimony to God's grace. God has blessed us time and again with influence, favor, connections, and finances. I began to see God's hand on us as a church and on me as a pastor. God is doing countless good things all around us if we take the time to look.

So where am I today? My church is still small. But half the people in the church were not connected to faith or to a faith community before joining ours. I appreciate where we are and the relationships I am able to have with everyone who comes. I'm still overweight, but I am in a wonderful fitness cohort with other pastors and am addressing my health. I am also engaged—to a marathon runner no less. She has me running a 5K this spring! I still have dreams, goals, and hopes. Now I have a plan, a strategy, and a healthy balance of expectations and realities. Looking back, I am a better pastor, a better leader, and truthfully a better follower of Christ as a result of these experiences. I don't think God put the roadblocks in my path; I think God used and is using them to grow me, mature me, and get me to depend less on myself and more on him. I'm still seeing Mark, still on the antidepressants, and still have bad days. Now, though, bad days don't turn into bad weeks, failures don't result in despair, and I'm not God in my own or in anyone else's life. God is.

RYAN BEATY is the Founding Pastor of VillageHouston in Houston, Texas. An ordained Assemblies of God minister, he is passionate about reading good books, developing leaders, and supporting Houston sports teams. He holds the MDiv from Assemblies of God Theological Seminary and a BS in Church Ministry from Southwestern Assemblies of God University. Sometimes described as "endearingly awkward," he can often be found at the local indie movie theater, perusing record stores, or trying out a new restaurant while *always* wearing a pair of Chuck Taylors. A bi-vocational pastor, he spends his days joyfully serving as chaplain at an Episcopal day school.

2

Our Time Is Now: The Impact of Assumptions on Young Pastors

Michelle Bodle

"We know she looks like she is sixteen, but this is our pastor."

I have been at my current parish for a little over a year now, and it is still common for members to introduce me to new people this way. Standing under five feet tall, I know I look young for my age. My mother keeps telling me that it will be to my benefit someday, but right now I simply feel that it erodes my pastoral authority. The first time I remember hearing the word "ageism," I was in the "Religion and the Social Process" class in my first year of seminary. While I had grown up learning about racism and sexism, the concept of age discrimination was new to me. Most of our class discussion centered on prejudices against the elderly, but in only a few short years this word took on a new meaning for me—prejudice against youth.

In most careers, young people are viewed as vital assets, new blood with new eyes for an ever-changing world. Yet in the church this does not seem to be the case. While my particular denomination laments the fact that only about 6 percent of their current clergy are under the age of thirty-five, this concern does not trickle down to the local church. With so many churches being served by second-career pastors and those nearing retirement age within the next ten years, a young face is not normative. There once was a day and age when young people were nurtured in their call and attended seminary directly following college, sometimes even serving congregations while simultaneously pursuing their degrees. But this is no longer the case. As a result, when a young clergyperson who did follow a sequential degree path is presented as the new pastor of a congregation, assumptions abound.

Assumption 1: Young clergy will bring in youth and young adults. A dirty little secret, a stereotype really, never discussed in seminary is that young clergy are only good with young people in the eyes of a congregation. But as someone who does not have the gifts or skills necessary for youth ministry, this was hard for me to believe. While I do have young clergy friends who are wonderfully graced in the area of youth ministry, I am not among them. I do, however, passionately teach and serve college students—just not in the way that many congregations probably imagine or envision at first.

Young clergy cannot by mere virtue of their age reverse the growing trends of the national church. David Kinnaman's book, *You Lost Me: Why Young Christians are Leaving Church and Rethinking Faith*, contains heart-breaking statistics collected by the Barna Group. More than 43 percent of young churchgoers drop off in attendance between their teen and young adult years.[2] Most faith switches happen between the ages of eighteen and twenty-nine.[3] The church is obviously missing the boat. But placing a young clergyperson in an aging congregation that yearns for a revival of the 1950s, when people flocked to open church doors, is not the solution. Kinnaman writes, "Young leaders who speak the language of their peers are sorely needed because today's twentysomethings are not just slightly or incrementally different from previous generations. Mosaics are living through *discontinuously different* social, technological, and spiritual change."[4] I fully agree with him. However, young clergy must be allowed to reach out to other young adults in their own way and time. It is unrealistic to expect that simply by putting someone under the age of thirty-five in the pulpit, young people will flock to church as if such ministers are pied pipers. This is just a continuation of a 1950s notion of church growth.

For the past year I have led a weekly Bible study at the local university, which I also did in my last appointment. It is by far my favorite part of the week. I am blessed to build relationships with students and see their lives transformed for Jesus Christ. But I also know that most of those students will never darken the door of a church, whether mine or anyone else's. Some have been hurt by congregations, while others distrust religion in general. A lot of groundwork needs to be laid before young people will even consider coming to church. And more and more young religious leaders I know are asking if that's really what it's about anyway. Are we primarily called to get young adults into local churches or to keep youth from leaving the church? Or is it about helping them establish a deep relationship with Jesus Christ? This enduring process of building trust between younger generations and religious leaders, which requires patience, is not generally what congregations with young clergy have signed up for. The expectation, both spoken and unspoken, is immediate results in youthful attendance, but we live in a day and age where that just isn't possible.

Assumption 2: You need to be married to be an adult, and if you aren't married you can and should work all the time. This is particularly true for single young adult clergy. Through my career, my congregations expect me to be available to them at any time because I do not have a husband or children. While for most of my adult life I have viewed singleness as a gift, that notion has been seriously tried by well-meaning church folk who believe their life's mission is to set me up with a nice young man who, in the words of one woman, "can make my life complete." Yet I am no Rubik's Cube in need of solving. It is not uncommon to hear people tell me they are praying that I find a husband soon so I can be happy. That is the paradox of singleism. On one hand, the church likes that you are single because, in their mind, there is more justification for an expectation that you work all the time. On the other hand, they also bemoan that you don't have a spouse because it must mean that something is wrong with you. Singleism is discrimination against adults who are single. While I may not be an adult in the eyes of everyone I pastor, I am still a single adult of child-bearing age to most. So I am defective.

Last week I found myself angered by this absurdity that I cannot get around. I am usually not an angry person, but as I looked at my calendar, I felt it welling up deep inside me. My anger was associated with not being able to find time to go on a date because my calendar is overflowing with church-related responsibilities. It was anger that I can't spend time with my family because to so many people, since my family doesn't live with me and I'm not married, I must not have anyone else who loves me. I am a single, young clergywoman living in the middle of nowhere.

Ultimately, hanging out and dating is something I am interested in, so earlier this year I signed up for online dating. Let me tell you, it is not fun as a young clergywoman. You are immediately discredited by Christian websites because of Paul's infamous words in 1 Timothy. But on secular websites, I have run into two types of people: those wanting nothing to do with religion, which I represent, and those who are oddly attracted to me as a religious leader for less than holy reasons. Maybe it's part of my duplicity of serving in a conservative profession, but being politically liberal has led me to these supposed matches. Add that to the fact that I have a meeting or Bible study every night of the week and thus set an early Saturday bedtime to be at my best on Sunday, and the prospect of dating looks bleak. I can't escape the cycle of being single, so I am expected to work all the time and still not be an adult because I am not married. That makes no sense. Perhaps other young clergy have not faced this problem, and bless them if that is so, but my friends and I seem to have much of the same bad luck when it comes to dating, whether online or the old-fashioned way. Dating is complicated enough on its own without adding the pressure of people who want you to be married (or not married) because you are their clergy person.

Assumption 3: You don't know anything. I am a firm believer in the wisdom of elders, but I also know that I am not completely inept in my vocation or elsewhere. Youth does not automatically equal stupidity just as old age does not render one spontaneously wise. And if we were honest for a moment, young clergy usually get placed in small churches with lots of problems because many churches cannot afford to pay a seasoned, experienced pastor, which means that we must learn quickly on the job in pressure-filled situations that others don't experience. Never mind the fact that I have to have a master's degree for this job, or that the ordination board has grilled me for at least three years and found that I am a pastor who bears good fruit.

When facing people in the congregation who think you don't know anything, it can go one of two ways. People take you under their wing, coddle you, and try to teach you how it is (not how God wants it to be), or they speak harshly about your incompetence behind your back. What I have experienced most are people who tell you everything they think you are doing wrong to your face and expect you to change for their pleasure. I still remember having coffee with a church member who told me that I am a horrible preacher, as if that would be a helpful comment to any pastor. Sometimes it takes all I have in me not to set out on a path to prove myself to the congregation, as if there is actually a way to prove your pastoral identity and authority to others. I am wise enough now to know that every person I meet has different expectations, and even if I gave up everything on behalf of their whims, I still wouldn't be good enough in their eyes.

In the midst of these assumptions, how can any young clergy last? How can we find our pastoral identity? How can we stay true to our call? How do we learn the hard lesson of separating who we are as people from our roles as pastors? Most of the time I don't think I have any answers to these questions, but then I catch little glimpses of hope. People who refer to me as Pastor Michelle instead of only by my first name are an example. Having the courage to embrace who I am as a young adult and clergywoman in totality—rather than succumbing to change in order to appease the congregation—is critical for my sanity.[5] Asserting control over my schedule and life without feeling guilty is also key. It is hard to be a woman pastor, but especially a young, single one trying to live out the authority of the position with authenticity. I have tried just about everything to create a sense of respect. Wearing a collar. Wearing a robe. I know I have failed when people tell me how cute I look in them. I have gone the other route and worn clothes reflective of my style and age, only to be told I look inappropriate. At times I have believed that if I only work harder I will earn respect, and likewise if I only get to the next step in the ordination process authority will be guaranteed.

Nevertheless, I have learned that our pastoral identity and authority cannot be contrived or created by outward signs. True respect comes from embracing who we are in our call and living into it fully. It means understanding the assumptions that come with ageism but not letting them define us or our ministries. These are the things I wish someone would have told me in seminary. These are the things I wish my congregation would have been told: that I am not your previous pastor(s), nor will the pastor who comes after me be like me. I am simply me, no more and no less, called and appointed to this location based on prayer and gifting. I don't need to apologize for my age, and I also need not wear it like a hindering chain. I am simply the beloved of God called to shine the light of Christ in this particular place at this particular time. Authority and respect will come with time, not with a change in age, ability, or marital status. It will only come as the people get to know me and I get to know them and as we abide and grow together in the love of Christ. My age is not the salvation or hindrance the church wants to make it. And as young adults are not the future of American religion but rather a part of the body of Christ now,[6] so am I called to lead this particular body of Christ now with the entirety of who I am. It is my hope and prayer that young clergy will become less of an abnormality and more accepted for leadership in the church of Jesus Christ.

MICHELLE BODLE is an ordained Elder in the United Methodist Church serving a two-point charge in Central Pennsylvania. She holds the MDiv from Drew University's Theological School along with a certification in spiritual formation, and a BA in Religion and Psychology from Houghton College. In her free time she enjoys reading, cooking, and playing with her pet chinchilla, Marty.

3

Vocational Fulfillment in Christ Alone: Why Simply Working Harder Never Works

C. Taylor Sandlin

"Pastor," she said, "I wanted to let you know that some people have concerns."

Concerns? I had only been on the job a month. How could there already be concerns?

"They heard there was a wedding at the church on Saturday night by some non-church members," she continued.

I affirmed that there had been a wedding, but I wasn't sure why anyone would be bothered by it. Our church policy allowed non-members to get married in our church, even with another minister officiating, as long as they paid an extra fee. This couple paid the fee and left the sanctuary spotless. It was so clean on Sunday morning that I didn't even remember there had been a wedding the night before until this phone call. I admitted to the caller that I didn't understand what "some people" were concerned about.

"Well, I don't have a problem with it, but some people are concerned about colored people getting married in our sanctuary."

The phone was silent for a moment, as I was ill prepared for such blatant racism early on a Monday morning. "I am so glad that you don't have a problem with African Americans getting married in our church or even worshiping here with us," I said. "I don't have a problem with it either. I realize some people might. You let those people know that my office door is always open and all they have to do is drop by and I'll be glad to visit with them."

"Oh, okay," she said, and hung up.

I sat in shocked disbelief. I knew racism existed, but I didn't expect to see it in one of my most faithful church members. Anyway, who still uses the term "colored people"? What is this, the 1960s? (Although even then, it was still an inappropriate term in my eyes.)

In many ways, it was the 1960s, at least to my congregation, which was made up primarily of people in their seventies and eighties. The one Sunday school class aimed at non-senior adults had just six individuals, four of whom were in their sixties. That qualified them as the church's *young* adults! As far as many of the adults in my church were concerned, the best days of the church's life and the best days of the city's life were in the past. To them, the church's heyday was during the sixties when they saw nearly four hundred people in worship. Now they ran around a hundred. Most of them supported growing and moving forward, as long as moving forward looked a lot like going back.

But the church hadn't always looked so gray-haired. For decades a Veteran's Administration (VA) hospital provided the town's economic backbone. VA administrators and doctors, along with teachers from the local school district, provided a stable membership base for the church. When the hospital closed, though, much of the town did as well. By the time I arrived on the scene ten years later, the town had lost half its population and was coming apart at the seams. The people who remained consisted primarily of the poor who couldn't afford to relocate and retired professionals who had come to call this town their home and, whether for love, family, or simple economics, would stay in it until death.

This second group made up the bulk of my congregation. I knew the demographics going into the job, but at twenty-six years old and fresh out of seminary, I was undaunted by the statistics. I came to town excited for the opportunity, convinced that I was capable of accomplishing great things there. After all, I had excelled in seminary, and even had awards to prove it. My religious upbringing taught me to believe that if I just preached well enough, worked hard enough, and found the right ministry approach, I could change these people and this place for the good. In this church of senior adults, I knew that I would need to get well acquainted with doing funerals. What I didn't realize was how many funerals I would need to do to eulogize my own misconceptions of what it means to be a minister of the gospel of Jesus Christ! In order to survive all the Monday morning phone calls and persevere in ministry for the long haul, several myths I believed to be true needed to be put to death and buried. This was the only way that genuine gospel truths could be resurrected in me.

The first myth was that hard work—or, in spiritual terms, obedience to God's ways—always translates into good results. From an early age, I was taught that good things come to those who work hard at the tasks God has given them. Generally speaking, that lesson proved true for much of my life. I had a natural aptitude for school, so I worked hard at it, partly because I enjoyed learning and partly because I loved getting good grades. At every level of my education, I had worked hard, and good results followed. I expected my experience in the church to be the same. I set about my work with diligence, even developing a syllabus of sorts for the first three months of my pastorate complete with objectives, a reading list, and a detailed plan for what I would preach over the next quarter. Every three months, I would review my progress and make a new syllabus for the next three months. Within the first year, I made a home visit to every person in the church, hired a part-time youth minister to start a program for teenagers, and began a young adult class.

Six months in, we only had one youth attending our youth program. A grand total of eight adults had visited the new Sunday school class, but only two of them had stayed connected to the church in any meaningful way. These modest gains were completely overshadowed by the number of regular church members who had either died or moved into nursing homes. Regular attendance was down by a dozen people in a church that only ran a little over one hundred. One day my deacon chairperson entered my office and said, "My wife and I are leaving the church. It has nothing to do with you. We think you are the best thing to happen to this church, but we can't stay." Another deacon, Sam (not his real name), served alongside the deacon chair's wife on the property committee. When the woman dared to share her concerns about a decision the committee was making, Sam looked at her and said, "When we have a question about decorating the parlor, we'll ask for your opinion. Until then you can leave this to the men."

I was discouraged but not defeated. My journal is full of laments about the slowness of the progress, but I knew that good results didn't always happen on the first try. I still believed things could change if we simply added new people to the mix. I thought that all I had to do was work harder, so I added assignments to my syllabus. I joined several community groups that were trying to bring change to the area. I developed friendships with several African American pastors in town to model racial reconciliation. I joined a local civic organization in order to meet non-church members. I started a debate club at the school.

The church, for its part, also began to work a little harder. Instead of fixing an aging organ, they installed a new, colorful playground on the front lawn. They got over their fear of the building being messed up by outsiders and allowed me to open the church on Friday evenings so teenagers would have a safe place to hang out. Unfortunately, the only people who showed up to play games were senior adult church members. Most Sundays, the only child in the nursery was my own daughter. I visited prospects and asked what they were looking for in a church. When several unchurched neighbors said they were looking for a different kind of music than what our church sang, I believed them. I convinced the church to let me start a contemporary service. I enlisted help from surrounding communities. For the actual worship service, I hired musicians to drive down from the seminary each week. For publicity, I organized another group of college students to make my town a destination for a weekend mission trip. With slick brochures in hand, they canvassed every house in the city, inviting people to our new service. I ran advertisements in the paper and hung posters throughout town. I prayed and prayed. I did everything I could think to do . . . and no one showed—at least, no one new.

No one new showed up on the first Sunday, or the second, or any Sunday for the next three months. At that point, I sat in my office and wept. I had worked and worked and worked to no avail. Two years in, and I had nothing to show for my efforts. I had buried more church members than I had managed to add. I was out of energy. Worse, I felt like a failure, and for some reason, failure felt a lot like faithlessness. If you believe the myth that good work always leads to good results, then the absence of good results must mean you haven't worked hard enough or been faithful enough. The problem was that I couldn't work any harder. I just didn't have it in me. I looked at my self-made syllabi and thought, if I'm handing out grades, I must get an F. I knew if I were going to make it in ministry, I would have to find a new metaphor for success. The syllabi would have to go. When I finally admitted that I couldn't change the world by the sheer force of my good works, God's grace began to do a new work in me.

I found encouragement in the words of an older minister who had served at one of the largest churches in our state. Over supper, he explained how he had also been the minister at two other churches that had to close their doors immediately following his service there. I asked what he had done differently at the large church. He responded quickly.

Absolutely nothing. I worked as hard at the churches that died as I did at the church that thrived. So much in ministry is beyond our control: demographics, cultural shifts, life's circumstance, you name it. God's will is for us to be always faithful, but not always successful. We like to be successful. It certainly feels better than failure, but you can be both faithful and a failure, at least in the world's understanding of that term.

His words helped dispel the myth that anything done according to God's will must prosper. A quick glance at Scripture also affirmed this insight. Moses faithfully followed God and led the people toward the promised land. Jeremiah faithfully followed the Lord, and all he had to show for it was a funeral dirge. Peter preached the sermon of his life, and thousands were saved. Stephen did the same and was stoned for his efforts. All were faithful. All worked hard. Only some saw success.

Success is not an automatic result of hard work, even the hard work of obedience. Over time, failure after failure compelled me to bury the idea that hard work guarantees success. Like any burial, this one caused me much grief. Over the years, I had learned to place my self-worth, my value, in my ability to succeed. I realized that to bury this belief, I had to also bury the idol I had made of good results. It's not an easy thing to count our trophies as rubbish for the sake of knowing God, but when we do, we discover that Paul was right to say that none of our meager trophies, even the religious ones, compare to the surpassing worth of knowing Christ Jesus our Lord. For his sake, we lose all things, even our desire to succeed at changing the world.

In the place of striving for success, I learned to strive to know Christ. The good news is that I discovered I can know him in either success or failure. To do so, I had to change my gaze. A fellow pastor helped me make an adjustment one evening. I was complaining about all the big things that prevented my church from succeeding: demographics, decades of racism, economics. He looked at me and said, "Sounds to me like you're missing the trees for the forest. Why don't you take your eyes off the big picture and trying to find Jesus in the people right in front of you?" As I began to look for Christ, I found him. In that failure of a contemporary service, I saw his face in the senior adults who faithfully showed up each week, singing songs they didn't like because they believed me when I told them it would help. Some of those senior adults were true saints, praising Jesus long after the more obvious fruit of his kingdom had disappeared from their church's life. They were living examples of Habakkuk 3:17-18: "Though the fig tree does not bud and there are no grapes on the vines, though the olive crop fails and the fields produce no food, though there are no sheep in the pen and no cattle in the stalls, yet I will rejoice in the LORD, I will be joyful in God my Savior."

Similarly, I found Jesus in those African American pastors who knew a thing or two about being faithful no matter the circumstances. They had been serving this community long before I got there and would still be serving Jesus in that town long after I left. I found Jesus in the handful of new people who did show up to our church during those days. Their numbers never exceeded the number of those who died or moved away. No matter. For them, finding Jesus in that church changed everything. I learned to give thanks for that. I learned to find Jesus even in the lady who called me Monday morning about the wedding. Mainly because she didn't call back about that issue, but also because she kept serving our church in one way or another even after I'd gently called her on her racism. Jesus was still at work in her, thankfully, just as he was still at work in me.

I left that church for another one after a couple of years. It has continued to struggle to keep its head above water in a town that keeps falling apart. It has, though, hired the first female youth minister in its history. It has expanded ministries to the needy, helping provide water to an entire street that was without it. When my wife and I returned for a service five years after leaving the congregation, there were still only eighty people in attendance. Remarkably, though, ten of those eighty were African-American or Hispanic members who had joined since our leaving. Maybe it was not the progress any of us dreamed about, but it was progress nonetheless.

My next pastorate has had more successes, some of them fantastic successes, but I'm quick to realize that this has as much to do with demographics as with my preaching. My new ministry has had its share of failures, too. These have bothered me less than those I encountered in my first few years out of seminary. In those years, I learned to try and fail, to work and have it not work out, and still to find Jesus in the mess. I did that, in God's grace, by learning to look for Jesus not in the results of my ministry but along the way as I ministered. And that has made all the difference.

C. TAYLOR SANDLIN is the Senior Pastor of Southland Baptist Church in San Angelo, Texas. He holds the DMin and MDiv from George W. Truett Theological Seminary at Baylor University, and a BA in Speech Communication from Texas A&M

University. Affectionately known as "The Short Preacher," he has been published in the *Truett Journal of Church and Mission*, and enjoys spending time with his lovely wife and children.

4

Not Being King: Inheriting Unrealistic Expectations

Julian DeShazier

It is easy to forget that Martin Luther King, Jr. was a pastor. After all, his voice reverberated throughout American and then global culture, eventually transcending the pulpit in a lineage of prophets who have affirmed the regality of justice and mutual relations. It is certainly correct that King was more than a pastor, but he was indeed *a pastor*. Lest we forget that he wanted to be known and recollected as a minister of the gospel of Jesus Christ, and even as his roles grew from serving a congregation of 400 to becoming a shepherd for the American people, he was first, chronologically and essentially, a pastor. It is too bad, then, that this is not remembered more. King's article on Wikipedia (a site where history is made by the public, and then made public) has an intimidating lexicon of his work, or rather all of his work from the Montgomery Bus Boycott in 1955 and on. Barely mentioned in the retellings of his life are the facts of his serving as senior pastor of Dexter Avenue Baptist Church from 1954–1960.[7] This is important for our purposes not only because King has become a preeminent role model, regardless of denominational or political affiliation, but also because he left boots that are swallowing the feet of future church leaders. He is an overwhelming figure, and the church of his generation is equally overwhelming . . . and exciting, and frustrating. And their legacies have been both gold and patina for us.

Unrealistic Expectations

It wouldn't be helpful for me to tell my story—the story of a young pastor inside a venerable congregation—and leave aside the King bits. His legacy inspires and haunts me. I, too, grew up loyal to but largely unaffected by "church," especially the entertainment-driven, uncritically celebratory, and youthfully ignorant aspects of it.[8] I am only a pastor now because I believe that the church as an institution has defaulted on its debt to society, and complaining alone has never satisfied me. I, too, graduated from Morehouse College and had talents that lay beyond the pulpit: I'm a songwriter and rapper, and I took two years after Morehouse to lay the foundation for a career as *J.Kwest*.[9] I, too, *blah blah blah*—the comparisons end there—but when you're a smart, young black man inspiring people to greater action, there will be no shortage of attempts to create parallels. It is, in many ways, a deep and humbling compliment, but even more it is indicative of society's attempt to bring back what has been lost. I don't know what my parents and grandparents must have experienced—victories hard fought, won, then scaled back—but they are anxious for good leadership, and thrilled by even the first blossoms of a potential fig tree.

So when you come into a congregation, there will be an expectation. You are young, and smart, and preach different—but not too different—and you possess energy that the congregation desperately needs. Are they dying? Did half of them leave with the last pastor? You don't know (yet), but something happened to bring you there. Whatever happened wasn't the normal evolution of a progressing church. Most of them hire fifty-year-old white males until they can't anymore. Something happened. That means people like us usually enter into toxicity, and our arrival represents a deep and prophetic hope, a joy that resonates throughout the community.

When I saw the congregation so happy after I arrived, almost euphoric, I was excited for them but not for myself. Their level of happiness was directly correlated to their expectations of me, and they were pretty happy. I am the first black pastor and, at age 27 when I began, the youngest ever in the church's 116-year history. Plus, I rap. *You know all those kids who you say don't come to church? Sure, he'll bring 'em back.*

I'm not saying congregations are naïve, but they are so happy to have you—young and inexperienced as you may be—that often the conversation of *what really needs to happen* never happens. And when that conversation doesn't happen, you fall into whatever has ensnared the congregation in the first place (because *something* brought you there). Most seminary educations require enough family systems analysis to help us know that when we are caught up in a system, we fail to lead. Happiness subsides, and real work needs doing, and we get caught off guard.

When Dexter Avenue Baptist Church called King to serve as pastor, they were just exiting a tumultuous time with their former pastor and civil rights leader, Vernon Johns. They too were a venerable congregation, and most of their history tells the story of a people always willing to be on the cutting edge. King was intended to be a *departure* from Johns—a period of calm that would appease the church's silk-cloth tendencies; he ended up succeeding Johns in ways we couldn't have known beforehand. The point is, any congregation will have one set of expectations of you, and *God's will* may have another. When divine and human expectations coincide, you are, as Granny might say, "cookin' with grease." Either way, you should figure out what the congregation is expecting of your glorious arrival. (Perhaps remind them that Jesus' triumphal entry into Jerusalem was the beginning of his death). Let's put the palms down and talk details.

I asked my father what questions I should ask during my interview with the church. After all, I was interviewing them as much as they were interviewing me, right? (Wrong: most young pastors are taking the job opportunity if offered to them). My father said, "Ask them what a successful first year would look like for you as pastor." Before this, I had only trivial questions in my brain, nothing about expectations. ("Is there a parking space?") So during the interview I answered all their questions, and they wondered if I wanted to know anything (you know, about the parking space), and I said, "How would you fill in the blank? We had a great first year together because I, as your pastor, _____." And they stared at me.

Because the old myths of leadership say that's the question *I'm* supposed to answer: I'm the fixer. I'm Superman; I fix budgets and fill pews with young people. The expectations for most young pastors seem Christ-like. It isn't until we are forced to speak them aloud that we realize the extent of our dreaming and the height of our uncertainty. This is unfair to new pastors. The search committee at University Church told me, "We want you to bring young people back." They aren't foolish for that, but considering the situation of the church, it also wasn't a realistic one-year goal. We needed infrastructure. Previous pastoral leadership, capable and passionate as they had once been, had rendered committees inoperable; members would get a physical twitch if I asked them to help me do something (this is the toxic environment new pastors sometimes inherit). And we don't build without cleaning up the waste; we want a clean and firm foundation. So I can't add programming until we make progress on what remains broken. Plus, what would I look like coming in and immediately making large-scale changes? That disrespects the congregation's tradition and flies in the face of every good piece of leadership advice ever given.

I had just read Ron Heifetz's *Leadership on the Line: Staying Alive through the Dangers of Leading* before I began this new pastorate, and I was determined to spend my first year "on the balcony" looking at the "dance" of the congregation.[10] I had decided to add nothing for a year, no matter how restless I became, unless the thing that needed to change directly conflicted with the church's mission. Others have called this "exegeting the people," and the wisdom is clear: take time to get to know the system. Learn their names. Become their pastor. Locate the authority (if you think you're the one in charge, good luck!). Following this protocol helps to ensure that when it comes time to do the thing that must be done, you won't be doing it alone. As the first year went on, people in the congregation began to realize that the change they hoped for had a few steps worth noticing first. They were noticing with me that our worship and liturgy on Sunday did not adequately reflect our hope and faith. They could see more easily that the problem was not how we welcomed youth, but how we welcomed anyone at all (congregations that survive toxic situations become insular fast). We had to work on how our worship communicates who we are and what we believe, to God and to first-time visitors. This was the foundation.

I am three years in at University Church, and I can tell you that we are *just now* beginning to think about being an awesome faith community where young folks can discover God and themselves on their own terms. We *just* built a music studio and started partnering with others to expand programming. Things need updating. Upgrading. Strategizing. Praying over. Expectations don't always communicate that. In the old leadership myths, the history is yours to solve, not understand; the church hands you the keys and tells you what needs to be done. When King began at Dexter Avenue—as a 25-year-old serving in his first pulpit—he brought with him a 34-point plan to change the church. I'd be shocked if 25 of them weren't the result of expectations laid upon him by others.[11] In another instance, King was in the church basement conducting a meeting when he learned of his son's birth. As he heard the news, he rejoiced, named the child over the phone, returned to the basement, and finished his meeting—these were the expectations of the pastor.[12]

Up to now I've referred to these expectations as part of the "myth" of leadership, and I mean this intentionally.[13] Myths are not about fact or historical verifiability but about how people use them to create and shape meaning. The archetype of the "hero" or "savior" is a mythological creation, and our leaders are similar creations. We see them as heroes; they are without flaw, born gifted and blessed by the gods. They are blessed and should lead us. "Good leaders save the day," it is thought. If Sharon Parks is right in saying that good leadership is not inherent but can be taught, then the weak paradigms can and have been reinforced as well.[14] I am convinced that a poor construction of the "leader" myth endangers this next generation of the church far more than poor theology or poor integrity.

Living Down Expectations

The height of expectations isn't a sign of dysfunction; our religious words have always been loaded with "foolishness," and this is a virtue. It is good Christianity to see a miracle in a new opportunity, and part of the problem with the church nowadays is that our hope has been suffocated by realism. We are also fond of the traditional myth of the "leader" because those kinds of people were pastors when the church was healthy. It is a good inclination to want to revive God's church. What's wrong with the old model? *Are you trying to badmouth Dr. King?*

What my story, and the stories of many other young pastors, communicates is that our expectations are led by our insecurities much more often than our faith. It's not that expectations are unrealistic, but they can be unfaithful. Expectations, when informed by fear and not faith, are the most subversive forms of sabotage a young pastor can experience. You don't need to follow tradition; you need to be authentically you as God has created, called, and equipped you: if the tradition remains, it is because the Truth within it was resilient, and you forced nothing. It is essential to accept that you are going to disappoint someone's expectations of you. Letdown is not a sign of failure but the mark of a leader willing to fully engage the interior process. As much as that sounds like some "Jedi" teaching, you are going to disappoint someone. *You aren't moving fast enough. Change isn't coming at the rate I expected.*

Scapegoats are as old as Leviticus: don't take it personally. Congregations are living organisms, not monoliths, and they struggle just as humans do. That means they are happy to have you, and deeply hurting. You come in a time of great celebration and mourning. *You've come to fix problems—* or so the myth goes—that often have yet to be articulated. We humans are anxious creatures. Why would a room full of us be any different? This is advice I wish I had when I began. When people told me that I made the moon rise, I should have remembered the darkness below. When the congregation became increasingly anxious toward the end of my first year over the absence of a youth pastor, I should have preached (and practiced) the virtues of patience and discernment. But I didn't: I hired a youth pastor—one who, by no fault of her own, was not the right match. It was a leadership issue, and I fumbled. I succumbed to the anxiety and rushed to hire someone, anyone, who could save the day. My expectations were equally unfaithful.

The essence of every minister's call is to be faithful to God and to serve God's people: this is the heart of the Great Commandment.[15] But as much as the seminary degree can feel like a jetpack for a new world, we must avoid the "messiah complex." We can't do everything, and we certainly can't serve fear. Deconstructing the myth is easier said than done. We inherit these ridiculous expectations—both laypeople and clergy do—but do we recognize their source? Instead of living up to uncritical myths, how do we "live down" these expectations that come from our own anxieties? What can we expect of first-time pastors and still remain healthy, aggressive, and faithful?

The church has always welcomed charismatic and dynamic leadership, and, for better or worse, the polity of most churches is structured so that pastors always do the most. We're full-time workers, so that's understandable, but when the Protestant work ethic of Pastor King becomes the myth for all future pastors to follow, we are missing the point of a role model. The heroes of our past are meant to inspire us to do even greater (see John 14:12[16])—they are not meant to haunt us. Our congregations need to know as much.

JULIAN DESHAZIER is the Senior Minister of University Church in Chicago, Illinois. He holds the MDiv from the University of Chicago Divinity School and a BA in Sociology from Morehouse College. Known to many as "J.Kwest," he is also an award-winning musician and songwriter. He and his wife, Mallorie, are proud parents of their first child, a beautiful baby girl named Dania.

5

Waiting for the Church: One Lesbian Woman's Journey in Ministry

Jamie Lynn Haskins

I was a chubby kid, nonathletic, a bit awkward. So as you might imagine, sports were not my favorite leisure activity. Innocent games of kickball quickly became torture sessions. Each Wednesday at noon, my third-grade class lined up beside the baseball diamond, and the team captains selected classmates one by one. Every time a name was called, I'd feel a small amount of hope welling up inside that maybe the next name would be mine. Usually, however, it wasn't. And so, finally, when most kids had already been selected, I would trot over to join whatever team needed an additional player, feeling more than a little dejected and "leftover." Luckily, kickball is not the defining experience of my childhood. For the most part, it was filled with great love and joy. Overall, I was a happy young girl.

But as an adult I hold on to the memory of kickball, of squirming under the hot summer sun hoping to be chosen, waiting to be noticed, praying that someone might pick me, because I am a lesbian woman called to serve God's church. Yes, I am gay and called to ordained ministry, and with these two "truths" as part of my narrative, there are moments when I am yet again a chubby third grader standing outside the baseball diamond. I find myself again waiting, hoping, praying, yearning to be picked, to be chosen, all the time knowing that the odds of that actually happening are slim.

On the kickball field, I could understand why I had to wait, why I wasn't always chosen. I was clumsy, awkward, and unable to perform on a level equal to many of my peers. I get it. I simply lacked the abilities required for an athletic task. But this is where the comparison between my experience

of third-grade kickball and my journey to serve the church must come to
an end because I am *trained* to serve the church. I do have the requisite
skills for congregational ministry. I attended Vanderbilt Divinity School,
an excellent graduate school that prepares dynamic, passionate women and
men for ministry. I was mentored in the art of preaching and biblical study,
and my theological skills were honed and tightened. I was empowered and
equipped to provide pastoral care and to journey with people through both
great sorrow and great joy.

At least within the walls of Vanderbilt Divinity School, my academic
performance and demonstrated skill for pastoral ministry meant that I
was not left standing on the sidelines; I was not picked last. In the final
year of my Master of Divinity program, I was awarded a "Transition into
Ministry" residency, furnished by the Fund for Theological Education.
Because I showed great promise as a congregational leader and my mentors
had faith in my ability to shepherd and pastor God's people, I was placed
within a Seattle, Washington, congregation after graduation as the Minister
of Faith Formation and Social Justice for a two-year period. A cohort of
three fellow graduates was placed in congregations across the country, and
for two years we journeyed with one another through our first calls: first
funerals, first weddings, first sermons. All of the "firsts" of pastoral ministry
were shared with these peers as we slowly grew into our calling to congregational ministry and gradually came to understand what it means to occupy
the role of pastor.

I thrived in the congregation. As I offered my first children's sermon
during the second week of worship, with twenty diverse, engaged children
gathered around my feet, I felt my heart sigh in relief. I had found my
home. As we all joined hands to pray at the end of our time together, I
offered words to God and the children followed, and tears welled up in my
eyes because I knew, I simply knew, that this was my call. My residency
taught me that I loved serving the church. The congregation was my vocational call and home. This was where I was supposed to be, to live, and to
serve.

I wasn't naïve. I knew it would be difficult to get a congregational
placement within my denomination, the Christian Church (Disciples of
Christ), as an openly gay young woman, so a little less than halfway through
my residency experience, with more than a year to go in my placement, I
began circulating my papers through our denomination's "search and call"
system. As in many denominations, the first page of our ministerial profile,
right after the space for name and address, asks us to describe our "family

status." If you're heterosexual and married, you don't even have to think twice as you write about your spouse. This is what most congregations are looking for as they pour over ministerial profiles to select their next pastor. They imagine a happily married, probably male minister who will settle into a new call with his wife and children in tow. But if you're a lesbian, this portion of the profile is foreboding because you know that—no matter how qualified you are, no matter how many years of experience or education you have, no matter how deep and true your call from God may be—this "family status" portion of the profile, so prominently displayed on the first page of your paperwork, will forever keep you out of the running for the majority of church positions. And so prayerfully I filled out my ministerial profile, noting in the "family status" portion that I was in a lifelong, covenant relationship with my partner, a young woman also deeply committed to serving the church who currently found herself in an interim position. I then sent the papers on their merry way, into our denomination's system. And, like I have been doing all my life, I waited.

For the first four months or so, my other colleagues in the residency program did not circulate their own profiles. They were heterosexual and married, and so the search for a congregational placement probably wouldn't last as long for them. But then one day they too put their papers into the system, and for them, the calls from congregations searching for a pastor began coming, slowly at first but then rather quickly. We would touch base each week during our residency phone calls, and they would share that they were talking with a congregation that excited them, or they were on a second phone interview with congregation X and had two additional first conversations lined up for next week with congregations Y and Z. I was happy for my colleagues. They were incredible young pastors who were clearly talented and skilled. Any congregation would be lucky to have them. But I didn't receive phone calls. The interviews didn't line up neatly on my schedule. I waited.

I checked with several Regional Ministers in my denomination about the quality of my profile, and they assured me that it was excellent. My reference letters were strong. My questions were answered well. I was a dynamic candidate. Around this time, my colleagues began to enter into serious conversations with congregations, and as the final months of our residency positions loomed, they were able to imagine themselves in their new positions.

I loved the church. Every day of my professional life was music to my soul. I knew, deep in my bones, that I was doing exactly what I was supposed to be doing. But as the days ticked by, as the months came and went, I wasn't sure how much that really mattered anymore. I waited, yet again that chubby, nonathletic third grader squirming in discomfort under the hot summer sun, waiting to be picked.

Finally, calls from a few congregations did come. With less than two months left in my residency, I entered into serious conversation with one. I was one of two candidates in consideration. The congregation and I had shared many phone calls; they watched videos of several sermons, and I prayerfully discerned that if they called me as their pastor, I would go. I would uproot my life and journey with them, settling in a new state and making a new home, because I was being called to that community. And for a moment, I again felt that familiar hope growing within me. This was going to be my chance. Finally, I would be picked. This was my time. Then a phone call came. It was a member of the search committee. She knew she wasn't supposed to call me—that was the job of the search committee chair—but she simply had to call. She had to talk with someone because her heart was broken.

The search committee had just met to decide whom to call to the position, and after hours of conversation they had made the choice. While they thought I would be wonderful, that I was an excellent fit for the congregation and had many of the gifts they were searching for, they simply could not call me. I was gay, and the congregation "wasn't ready to deal with that yet." The woman on the other end of the phone was deeply upset. She was crying when she called, because her son was gay and she had thought her congregation would be more understanding, more accepting. Her tears came because she had been wrong. And so, there on the phone, she cried for herself, for her son, and for me. I was devastated. And though this member of the search committee had called me seeking pastoral care, my own heart was breaking, and so I recommended that she call her congregation's Regional Minister, and then I hung up the phone and cried.

At this point, all of my colleagues in the residency program had been chosen by congregations, but there I was, still waiting. It turns out that I would not be picked after all. And so I had to move on. I could not to wait to serve the church forever. My residency position was coming to a close in a matter of weeks, and I still had no idea what was next for me. My heart was in congregational ministry—I knew I was called to serve the church—but I also had to eat, and work, and support myself and my family. And so, with much grieving and mourning for the loss of what I had hoped would be, I began applying for college chaplaincy positions. I expected the silence, the waiting that I had come to know so well over the past year during my congregational search process. I prepared myself for more heartbreak. But within days of submitting my first résumé, the calls started pouring in. I received a call back from every single chaplaincy position for which I had applied. I was brought onto campus for last-round interviews twice within the first month. And within a quick five weeks, I had been chosen, out of a pool of more than 120 applicants, to serve as the Chaplain and Director of Spiritual Life at a small, liberal arts college in Missouri.

I have been in this position now for two years, and I am thriving and love it dearly. Just last week I offered the prayer and the benediction at our graduation ceremony. Following the service, several of my students came to give me hugs, to thank me for journeying with them, and as they turned to go, toward first jobs and new horizons, I again felt tears in my eyes. College chaplaincy is faithful, life-giving work, but the church I love, the denomination I had begged and pleaded to serve, never called my name.

It left me outside, standing, waiting to be chosen. Not because I wasn't called to serve God's people, not because I was not qualified, not because I wasn't good enough. It left me on the sidelines—dejected, unwanted, leftover—simply because I am gay. The church has the potential to be a place of radical inclusion and abundant hospitality. The church has the potential, but it is not there yet. And so, again, I wait.

JAMIE LYNN HASKINS is the Chaplain, Director of Spiritual Life, and Instructor of Religious Studies at Westminster College in Fulton, Missouri. She holds the MDiv from Vanderbilt University's Divinity School and a BA in English and Religious Studies from Stetson University. An alumnus of the Disciples Divinity House at Vanderbilt's Congregational Residency Program, she looks forward to the day when the denomination she loves, the Christian Church (Disciples of Christ), more fully reflects the diversity and beauty of all God's people. She lives with her partner, Sarah Klaassen, in Columbia, Missouri.

6

There Is No Union for Ministers

James Ellis III

As liberated as clergy in our twenties and thirties often strive to be, we are not that different from our predecessors. Consumed with budgets, baptisms, and buildings, like them we are prone to become power players in a religious institution rather than innovators of a sacred movement, pointing to and embodying Jesus' ways.[17] Worshiping at the altar of denominational (or nondenominational) politics, as proverbial chickens coming home to roost, young pastors are also guilty of choosing not to rock the vocational boat en route to influence and accolades. Yet it is not similar-aged colleagues with whom I have had unfortunate run-ins during these early years of ministry, but the so-called "old guard" instead.

Upon accepting a call to ministry, I committed to following God's sanctifying waters wherever they took me. I resolved myself to the fact that there would be unknown challenges, but I also knew that God was well qualified to fight on my behalf. After becoming a Christian at the age of twenty and later pursuing a life of ministry, I figured it was a no-brainer that any supervisors I encountered down the road would be morally upright, taking footsteps that I would be glad to follow. We're talking about ministry, right? Much to my surprise, however, I learned that not everyone in ministry has ministry *in* them, at least not to the degree I expected. I learned that developing one's authentic self, living within holy boundaries, and worshiping God—not money, power, or respect—aren't values intrinsic to all pastors. There is no union for ministers, and this is something I have come to know the hard way. Catholic historian John Dalberg Acton wrote, "Power tends to corrupt, and absolute power corrupts absolutely."[18] Unfortunately, this maladaptive paradigm is more normative in church leadership than we care to admit.

Prior to the stories that follow, I served two churches. First, I served a Baptist congregation in Gaithersburg, Maryland, where I was as interim youth minister for six months. A few years later, after getting married and beginning at George W. Truett Theological Seminary at Baylor University, I was hired by a United Methodist church in Temple, Texas, to serve as youth pastor, which I did for almost two years. There I had a great group of middle and high school students to minister to and with, and a congregation that graciously supported my graduate studies. I burned candles at both ends, commuting multiple times each week as a full-time student and full-time pastor. All this is to say that I wasn't *green* about ministry's nuances. I knew it was tough work, full of regularly encountering people, parishioners mostly, who had lots of complex issues in their lives. But overall, I had very positive experiences at these two churches. They both had solid leadership at the pastor level and with the laypeople, and were well managed, which interestingly enough left me unprepared for the melodrama I would encounter at other places. Also, in most of my seminary coursework we rarely discussed *real* conflict—the kind that is messy, unpredictable, and jarring.

Act I: When You Don't Fit

After completing my second master's degree at Pittsburgh Theological Seminary, with a recession in full swing, after five months of searching I finally began working at a historically black, all-male college in Atlanta, Georgia. I was hired as associate campus minister, a new position funded by an external grant. From the beginning, my wife and I had our concerns about whether it was a good match. The compensation was well below what we had hoped for, especially at an institution that in certain circles was lauded in higher education's "black Ivy League." We also had doubts about whether doing ministry in a context so heavily steeped in pageantry and liberal exclusivity would suit me. The dean of the chapel, who would be my supervisor, had been at the college in that same position (as the only person to hold it) since the year of my birth. And I was thirty-one years old at the time. In Maryland and Texas, I'd been the first person of color to join the staff of both previously mentioned, predominately white churches, so I wasn't easily frightened by a challenge. Moreover, as a black man, the opportunity to guide other young black men was appealing. My hopes were high. Though we had concerns, my wife and I could see potential. After discussing the pros and cons (no doubt influenced by looming student loans and other bills, alongside an eagerness to move on with post-seminary life) we decided to make a go of it, to take a leap of faith.

But after barely ninety days, I was summoned to an impromptu meeting with the dean of the chapel and the chief financial officer, where I was informed that, effective that day, I would no longer be retained. No allegations of impropriety, slothfulness, or insubordination were levied against me. I was simply told that it was felt that I was not a good fit for the position. That was it. While disappointed, I can't say that I was stunned by the news. Almost as soon as I'd begun in the position, I sensed that the college's ways and means, and the dean of the chapel's larger-than-life presence, might prohibit me working there long-term. But I was determined to put my best foot forward. Regrettably, it was tough going from the start. The chapel department said funds weren't available to cover a final in-person interview, so we only had a phone interview. Expenses for our 643-mile relocation were barely covered. My paychecks were routinely incorrect, sometimes taking weeks to be fixed, and let's not even get into similar issues with my benefits coverage. In youthful dialect, it was a "hot mess."

In the aftermath of my dismissal, I heard countless objections from other staff members not only about the unfairness of my situation but also about how the dean of the chapel's stronghold on the department had negatively affected the quality of pastoral care and leadership offered to students. Over the next few months, I was informally told of a few reasons that I was let go. I'd failed to embrace the college's unspoken values, and I had also failed to worship the dean of the chapel's scholastic tutelage and sage wisdom. I am guilty of all that. Behind closed doors, the dean of the chapel was condescendingly referred to by many students, faculty, and staff as "the dean." To them, he had morphed over three decades into more of a religious than pastoral figurehead, offering lengthy invocations, presiding at coveted ceremonies, writing recommendation letters for students and alumni in his good graces to pursue graduate theological education, and hobnobbing with dignitaries and prominent Atlanta clergy. In the short time that I was there, conversely, I'd established a very different identity, connecting with students in the dorms, at campus and community events, and via social media and such—simply trying to encourage and counsel students.

When he wasn't away traveling (which he did often), the dean of the chapel and I had what I thought were positive conversations about my performance. I never got the impression that I was stepping on his or anyone else's toes. Even so, I was well aware that I was not like many alumni and college employees in how I behaved and thought. During an uncharacteristically frigid winter, heat in the chapel office stopped working. We were still required to report to work, however, so I brought along a small space heater from home. After it ran for maybe fifteen minutes, with fellow staff now huddled around my desk trying to keep warm, power to the entire building suddenly went out. Mind you, we are talking about a 2,500-seat auditorium and multilevel building with numerous offices. Maintenance eventually arrived, and after some time poking around, they pointed to my teeny-tiny heater as a possible cause of the outage. I was told that this kind of thing was pretty normal because of outdated wiring. The dean of the chapel was out of the office, so in his absence I suggested to other supervisors that we work from home until the heat was restored. Thankfully, the request was granted, but I can only presume that some higher-ups may have felt that I wasn't "paying my dues" or showing the college its customary level of obligatory devotion. But cold is cold and sick is sick, and I get sick when I am cold.

In that respect, while I enjoyed reaching out to students, I definitely was far from being in awe of the college or dean of the chapel. An expert on the college's history and its famous graduates, having outlasted a score of college presidents through the years, he'd brokered into a position of virtual carte blanche. He didn't use e-mail, which made communication a nightmare. The college's solution was for staff members to print any correspondence that needed to be shared with him, slip it underneath his office door, and pray that he responded in a timely manner, which rarely happened.

Being let go the way that I was hurt. I wish I'd been allowed to finish the academic year. But every opportunity isn't for everybody, I've learned, regardless of how one's cultural, racial, or educational background may match stated goals or needs. Incongruity or dysfunction can bubble beneath the surface of any opportunity, the iceberg-sized pieces of which you only see face to face once you are actually swimming in the ocean.

Act II: When Insecurity Reigns

Having accepted an associate pastor appointment through the regional United Methodist conference, the next stop on this doozey of a journey was the oldest town in West Virginia. A stone's throw from Maryland, Virginia, and Pennsylvania, Shepherdstown is full of rolling hills, farmland, and Civil War landmarks. I and three other young clergy were selected for a new project that would fund our placement as associate pastors in four African American churches. As an ordained Baptist minister, my ordination was recognized, but I was considered "on loan" and thus without permanent standing in the United Methodist Church. Having just endured one tough situation, I was in no hurry for another. From all that we could see, my wife and I felt that this opportunity would be a good one. And despite what I will share next, I thoroughly enjoyed introducing and reintroducing some wonderful people there to Jesus. After a few months on the job, however, I began observing things about the senior pastor, my supervisor, that I knew were likely to put us at irreconcilable odds. In about eight months, the program had failed, and I'd been terminated. Talk about *déjà vu.*

In the first few weeks of work, my wife and I began building relationships with anyone and everyone. Although an associate pastor, I tried to connect with the entire congregation and community. My wife began leading a community-based small group for women that quickly took off. Many women who had become disenfranchised with that particular church or with Christianity in general began finding solace in the group. Through social media, sermons, and other means, I built bridges to nearby college students and young adults. In casual conversations, they'd confess that they enjoyed my preaching because it somehow made the Bible come alive to them. And since I rarely preach longer than twenty minutes, they expressed appreciation that, though creative, my sermons were to the point. They were grateful that I respected their time and treated them as if I believed they were intelligent. This was, however, in stark contrast to the senior pastor's preaching style, so it's easy to see how tension brewed as congregants and even visitors of all ages began inquiring if I could preach more often.

In the relationships that my wife and I built, we treated people like we were truly interested in their lives and wanted to journey with them no matter if they did or did not regularly attend worship or give financially. That will always be our approach: love the heck out of people, get to know them, and through relationship and teaching try to show them the details of a life of faith in Jesus. But this wasn't anywhere close to the kind of philosophy that the senior pastor and his wife, who was also very involved in the church, had about ministry. I think it's fair to say that he was never really adopted[19] by the church, even though by this time he'd been there for about seven years. That tends to happen, however, if you berate people's sociocultural history and seem conniving. He expended most of his energy trying to move older members out of the way, while making it no secret that he desired and deserved, he would say, a "better" appointment.

About halfway through my employment, I began summarily receiving criticism from him. Overnight almost, my ministry to college students and young adults was characterized as inadequate, and he levied that I wasn't contributing enough to the congregation's overall productivity. One criticism led to another and another, which elevated to meetings with conference-level staff. And before long I was let go. The conference offered a severance package consisting of an abbreviated salary and benefits for a month or so. The catch, however, was that it required signing a document stating that I agreed to cease all contact with the congregation. The conference said this was a good-willed gesture of concern for my family's well-being. But we weren't buying it. In our eyes, hush money is hush money no matter what you call it, so we rejected their offer, instead trusting that God would honor our integrity. I later discovered that the year prior to my arrival, the church had hired an associate pastor who lasted only a few months more than I did, his time concluding with a similar series of criticisms from the senior pastor.

Although I hate that it is true, as ravenous wolves (Matt 7:15), some pastors, regardless of age, aren't in ministry to help people so much as to secure their piece of the upwardly mobile pie. Like yesteryear's Israelites, they manipulate people because they first have been led astray (Isa 9:16). Early on, the senior pastor would warn me to steer clear of certain people and whole families in the church whom he viewed as troublemakers. Reflecting on it now, his behavior was that of paranoid psychosis; he would go on and on about this bad person or that bad family who, in his words, refused to accept his authority. Yet I never once had a problem with anyone, and especially not any of the people whom he thought were bad apples. If anything, the more I extended myself to them and other *excommunicated* congregants, the more quickly they became the biggest supporters of the work that my wife and I were doing. I am sure this dynamic only spurred his passive-aggressive antics. Given the research of Dean R. Hoge and Jacqueline E. Wenger, as presented in *Pastors in Transition: Why Clergy Leave Local Church Ministry*, mine wasn't an isolated incident:

> . . . many associate pastors reported difficulties with their senior pastors. Some of them told us that their senior pastors were controlling or micromanaging; others said the senior pastors were unaccustomed to having an associate and did not welcome them; still others told of staff members

whose personal issues affected all their colleagues. Associates told us that they often felt unable to control their lives because they were too much subject to the whims of the senior pastor.[20]

I do not wish my experiences on anyone, but I'm better for them (see Jas 1:2). More than being a pastor, I am first a follower of Christ. I find solace in knowing that integrity matters to God, and Christians and non-Christians alike desperately need to see it lived out, especially in unfriendly, unfair situations.

Act III: Choosing to Keep the Faith

Known especially for his best-selling Bible translation, *The Message*, Eugene H. Peterson is a retired Presbyterian (PCUSA) pastor and dynamo in the field of pastoral theology/leadership. Some months ago we began corresponding via phone and letter, and I learned that he is just as captivating, down to earth, and wise as his many books suggest. The candid, countercultural witness of his multifaceted ministry has been manna to me. In our first few phone conversations, after sharing these ministry transitions that I have recently endured, he said something that I'll never forget: "Oftentimes, the biggest difficulty of being an associate pastor is the senior pastor . . . and unfortunately we don't live in a society that honors the things you're seeking to honor, James. Sadly, that is true in many of our churches today also, as you have already experienced."

The pastoral life is stressful enough without superfluous glitches, but any vocational cookie can crumble unexpectedly, right? Yes, but ministry is something a bit different. We can (and often do, I find) have just as much or more education and experience as peers in other professions, but we will seldom receive commensurate compensation. We regularly field frantic inquiries from congregants and strangers who seek help, and we risk life and limb to assist however we can. We wrestle with the arduous tasks of proclaiming God's word through sermons, Bible studies, prayer, and small groups while simultaneously offering pastoral care and leadership through visitations, weddings, funerals, baptisms, community service, and countless meetings about everything from bequeaths to bathroom renovations. It is at times thankless work only exacerbated by discordant employment. Romanticizing or spiritualizing vocational ministry is unwise. Like anyone else, clergy sometimes *just* need a job. Take it or leave it, call me blasphemous if you will, but it is true. We don't live in a spiritual vacuum. We have bills to pay and can't sit in monastic solitude waiting for a cloud of incense to lead us to the pastoral post of our dreams. Everyone hopes their next position is a harmonious, enduring match for their gifts and skills, but that doesn't always happen. Believe me, I know.

In both of my situations, I had good reasons to believe that the new context for ministry could be a good fit for me. Even to the extent that there were some good concerns, I still had to feed my family. Therefore, while not outright ignoring any information, my wife and I[21] decided to leap into the vortex of uncertainty called faith in those moments. In a different time, under different circumstances, I might've never accepted the two aforementioned positions. Having had two or three other suitable offers to ponder, I may have chosen another path. But maybe not. I will never know. Despite how things turned out, I'm confident that God sent me to each of these places for good reason. None of it was easy, but I did learn a lot about faith, ministry, people, and myself—more than I would have otherwise. Conflict and injustice have a way of pushing you to reassess what means the most for your life.

Let me be clear. These transitions caused a real crisis of faith and vocation for me. I felt forsaken by God at times, upset that wrong had outwardly been allowed to prosper at my expense. But while grieving the loss of what I had hoped, in time I was reminded that God's plans for me were and always are good (Jer 29:11). With support from my wife, mentors, and friends, I found recalibration and renewal: "Let us not become weary in doing good, for at the proper time we will reap a harvest if we do not give up" (Gal 6:9). I pray often that I never become a minister hungry for power, relegated to treating people as mere objects to be manipulated for my benefit. Ministry is not a number's game or political telethon to me. It's not a competition wherein the person with the most power or strategy wins. Ministry is about *helping* hurting people in Jesus' name, in Jesus' ways, in Jesus' power.

Given my pastoral sojourn, it's sobering to know that I will one day answer to Jesus for the quality with which I have shepherded his sheep (John 21:16; 1 Pet 5). Today I *choose*—and it is a choice—to "lead with a presumption of grace."[22] I hope for and expect the best from those entrusted to lead me. Yet I'm absolutely more intentional and thorough now about asking pointed questions of search committees and others when considering employment opportunities. As they interview me, I interview them like nobody's business. Co-laboring with people who are humble, committed to integrity, and striving to honor God is by far the most important component of my evaluation.

Unlike some profressions (professional athletes with their collective bargaining agreements, the screenwriters' guild, teachers' unions, etc.), there is no union for ministers. That fact just comes—or rather does not come—with the territory. However, instead of chasing after power and wielding it recklessly, we who are *called* are to leverage our positions for the betterment of the vulnerable. We are not legislators with clerical collars. We are to be humble servants. "There is a price to pay for speaking the truth," says Union Theological Seminary's esteemed professor Cornel West. "There is a bigger price for living a lie." I can tell you firsthand that evil is as active behind the scenes of ministry as anywhere else, and youth doesn't provide an exemption from the tragedy that often results when evil is allowed to thrive. But I can also tell you about God's faithfulness, which cannot be bought but only freely received from the giver and sustainer of life.

JAMES ELLIS III is an ordained Baptist pastor and writer based in the District of Columbia, who holds the Master of Sacred Theology from Pittsburgh Theological Seminary, the Master of Theological Studies from George W. Truett Theological Seminary at Baylor University, and a BA in African American Studies from the University of Maryland. He loves spending time with his wife, and, as a former "spoken word" poet, is the author of *OnThaGrindCuzin: The School Daze of Being "Incognegro" in 1619* (PublishAmerica, 2004).

7

Tales from the Interview Process: Unhealthy Search Committees and Churches

Chris Thomas

It was the spring of 2009, and I could see the proverbial light at the end of the tunnel. Along with some of the final research papers and reading assignments of my seminary courses, my home printer was noisily spitting out several copies of my résumé (on premium, 100% cotton résumé paper, of course). The "sent" folder of my email account was filled with messages to enigmatic addresses like "pastorsearch@baptistchurch.org" with electronic copies of my résumé and .mp3 files of sermons attached. The ministry placement employee at my seminary had both hard and electronic copies of my résumé, with my understanding that it would be going out to churches in the area as soon as they requested them. I had even sent my résumé to state Baptist leaders in several states and to friends and colleagues whom I thought might have contact with search committees during their travels. I wanted to be sure I had all my bases covered so that I could kick back while the letters, emails, and phone calls from search committees came flooding in during my summer mentorship.

But there was no kicking back, and responses from search committees flooded in the same way rains flood the Mojave Desert in July. Occasionally, I'd receive a letter in the mail from a church of which I'd never heard, and they always said about the same thing: "Thank you for sending your résumé, but we feel that God is leading our church in a different direction." There came a point when I learned that a letter with the return address of a church was not a letter bearing good news for my vocation. Then, one day, I didn't get a letter—I got a phone call.

It was from the chair of a search committee in south Alabama. His voice was laced with the mixture of attempted professionalism and casualness that is familiar to those of us raised in the Deep South. He proceeded to tell me about the size of the church building, how much they wanted to grow, and how desperately they wanted a good pastor. He was quick to point out that they could offer a parsonage for my wife and me (though our cat would have to stay outside, preferably on a leash!). They would inspect the parsonage every six months, and any repairs or updates would be made at my expense. He wasn't exactly winning me over at this point. He made his way back to talking about the new sanctuary they built a few years ago and how it could seat over four hundred people. So I asked the obvious and inevitable question: "Well, how many do you usually have in attendance on a Sunday morning?" The response shocked me a bit: "On a good Sunday, we'll have about thirty or forty." Alarms sounded in the back of my brain. After our conversation ended, I talked to my wife, and we decided that this church was obviously not where we were supposed to go, so we continued to wait.

There were a few more letters, an email or two, and a questionnaire that I returned to a church I never heard from again. But then came another phone call. This time the call came from a church in northeastern Alabama. There were two men on the other end of the phone, and they told me about their church and how they would be happy to send me more information about it, including copies of the budget, recent bulletins, and the latest newsletter. They seemed open about the church's circumstances and were already planning on flying my wife and me out to meet them. During a follow-up phone conversation, I got down to asking the questions we hate asking about church (you know, questions about numbers, salaries, etc.). That's when things started getting a bit shaky. I asked, "How many people are in attendance on an average Sunday?" Their response was one I had heard a few times before: "Well, *if everyone was here*, we'd have this many . . . ." While I was in seminary, during my time as pastor of a small, rural church, I learned that when a pastor or church member says "If everyone was here we'd have this many," it means you can safely divide the number by two and have a more accurate statistic. With that in mind, when they told me, "If everyone was here, we'd have about a hundred," I knew I could safely assume they averaged about fifty or sixty in worship each week. I followed up one ugly question with another: "What are you willing to offer in terms of compensation?" This was the nicest way I knew how to ask, "How much are you able to pay me?" Their response: "We were thinking $42,000 to $45,000 a year."

Here is where I think search committees need a little training. If potential candidates ask how much a congregation is willing to pay, don't give them a range of hard numbers. Of course they will want to be compensated with the higher figure, and if they are offered the lower figure first it sends a message that they aren't exactly the people you had in mind as a first choice. I have found it works best to offer one solid figure and allow for negotiation.

In asking about the salary, I found out that I would not be offered any benefits; I would be responsible for purchasing my own health insurance and contributing to some sort of retirement program without any additional funds from the church. I would also have to handle my own deductions, paying taxes at the self-employment rate. I was told further that the church had five other staff members. You read that right: five other staff members for a church of fifty to sixty people. I was reassured, however, that the other staff members were paid out of a trust fund left by a member many years ago for the explicit purpose of paying staff salaries (I quickly learned that this was not true at all). In the end, the church offered me a package that totaled $44,500 per year, which I later found out was uncomfortably close to (and practically less than) the salary of an untrained staff member. I was told that particular staff member only made $28,000 per year, was loved by everyone in the congregation, and was excited about the prospect of a new pastor. I eventually learned that every one of these statements was untrue: he made $42,000 per year (with the church paying for his health insurance and its portion of his taxes, etc.), he was loathed by the congregation because of his arrogance in leading worship in a style that did not suit them, and he himself wanted to be the pastor. These truths revealed only a few of the misleading words from the search committee.

I had also asked for a copy of the church's bylaws: I had determined that I would not serve a church that did not have bylaws, because a church without bylaws is vulnerable to corruption. At first, I was told the church had bylaws, but they so rarely used them that someone would have to find a copy to send to me. When I pressed the issue during a face-to-face interview with the committee, I was told something entirely different: it turns out the church did not actually have any bylaws, but I was quickly reassured that if I was called as their pastor, the church would be willing to go through the process of creating bylaws. This was presented to me as a sort of compromise. I was also asked about issues regarding music styles,

Bible translations, and who could and could not hold leadership positions within the church. I answered every one of these questions as honestly as I could, even though I was certain some of my answers would be unpopular and might actually cost me the job. Despite my honest answers, the search committee decided I was the candidate they'd like to present to the church.

After flying out and meeting the committee and touring the church building, my wife and I felt that the church was a fine place to serve (especially since it would bring us back to our home state). Now, if I am being honest, I did not receive any sort of "sign from heaven" that this was the church God was calling me to serve. The signs were a bit more, shall we say, practical: there were no other churches calling, and my wife and I had to be out of the house we had been renting during my time in seminary by the end of the summer. So, in the weeks that followed, we flew to Alabama, where I "preached in view of a call" and received an overwhelmingly positive vote from the congregation (only five members voted "no."). When I arrived back in Texas, I announced my resignation to the church I had been pastoring, and my wife and I began packing up our house.

The first few weeks of any new ministry venture can be challenging. You have new names and faces to remember. You have to learn and relearn the location of the nearest Walmart and hospital. You have to find a place to live. Then, on top of all this, dump the stress of pastoring a church that looks nothing like the church presented to you by the search committee that nominated you. In my first weeks as the new pastor, I learned several important lessons. The most important was this: there are some church members and search committees that will say whatever it takes to put a warm body in the pulpit. An unreasonable sense of urgency drives some search committees to present outdated information, bend the truth, or even flat out lie.

In those first weeks as pastor, I learned that the church had no interest in ever creating bylaws (I was told so by a deacon who had even served on the search committee!). I learned that the five staff members were not hired and paid for because of a fund left my a former member: rather, they were hired so no member would have to volunteer to do the work, and the previously mentioned fund was actually a source of frustration and division in the church, used by members connected to the benefactor to guilt and persuade other members in the church. Moreover, I discovered discrepancies in information regarding the other minister on staff, particularly his lack of training, his much higher salary, and his relationship with the congregation. There were also issues concerning which translation(s) of the Bible I used: a member of the search committee was a firm believer in the King James Version being the only inerrant word of God, and when it became clear that I would not use that version—after I had stated in an interview with the committee that I would not—he and his wife left the church!

After about six months, I felt it was necessary to call the search committee together to discuss my time at the church to that point. I voiced my concerns about the differences in the church they presented to me and the church I was currently pastoring. I specifically mentioned the harsh rejection of bylaws and the relationship between the associate minister and the congregation (it was about this time that he actually resigned, having secured a position with another church). The members of the committee kept their responses to a minimum, but then the chair said something that no pastor or pastoral candidate should ever hear from a search committee member. He looked me right in the face and said, "If we had told you the truth, you wouldn't have wanted to come."

Now, understand that he did not say those words with shame, guilt, or desperation. No, he said them with a tone that conveyed a sense of finality. It was as if he told me, "We did what we had to do to get you here, and now that you're here, you can't do anything about it." I felt helpless. I felt hoodwinked. I felt trapped. What could I do? I had only been a full-time pastor for six months. What would it say to another search committee who saw that on my résumé? How could I possibly present my case to another church without sounding like I was simply trying to find a "better job"? Should I just suck it up and play the cards that were falsely dealt to me?

I consulted some of my older friends in ministry. Most of them wrote it off as a lesson better learned now than later. Others said I should stick it out for a few years, so it wouldn't look as bad on my résumé. A few suggested sending my résumé out again right away. I listened to all of them. I definitely learned to be more cautious and questioning when interviewing with search committees. I did wind up sticking around for about three years, but I reactivated my résumé after the first year. It took two years before I got another call from a search committee.

I hope my experience with deceptive or misleading committees is rare, but I have a terrible feeling it is not. I do, though, think I understand where it comes from. You see, when a pastor leaves a church (whether he or she resigns, retires, or is terminated), the congregation can go into a sort of panic, especially if that pastor has been there for a while. A healthy congregation can recognize the importance of a prayerful, thoughtful, and well-planned process. In a healthy congregation, people are intentional about the way they promote the church and the kinds of candidates they are willing to consider. The process will take longer, but in the end, it has the potential to create a high-functioning, long-lasting ministerial relationship. Unhealthy congregations, however, go about things quite differently.

An unhealthy congregation allows the panic of a sudden pulpit vacancy to drive the search process. They feel the need to fill the pulpit as soon as possible. Some will see the interim period, however brief, as a time to correct problems they saw in the former pastor (lowering the pastor's salary, moving the pastor's office, requiring office hours, etc.). They will take shortcuts in order to speed the process along. They assume that whomever they call as their next pastor will count it as a blessing to serve, and he or she will have to adjust to the congregation rather than the both parties mutually adjusting to one another as people do in any other relationship.

It has been my experience that these unhealthy churches rarely call successful pastors. What I mean is that it seems they rarely, if ever, call ministers in their prime: ministers with training, experience, and expertise that the congregation will actually heed. Rather, it seems they either call ministers who are on the verge of retirement, those with little formal training, or young ministers, especially those of us right out of seminary. For young ministers, these churches are often the only ones interested in talking to us. They tend to see us as a "bargain," as pastors with expensive educations who are willing to accept whatever salary package they offer. Plus, there is a terribly misinformed myth that a young minister will attract young families. These unhealthy churches often see young pastors as a "quick fix": someone who will do an adequate job preaching and teaching while simultaneously taking a low salary and attracting the young people who've been missing from the pews for years.

Thankfully, my vocational journey did not end with the experience I have described above. During my last two years, my résumé made the rounds again. This time I was able to be a bit more discerning and patient. I interviewed with several churches, even turning down a couple because they felt too much like my experience right out of seminary. I wound up accepting the call from a church not too far from where I was serving. I know I would not be there now if I had not gone through the experience I have described.

I wish I could have avoided the deception. I wish congregations could be more open about their situations with potential pastors. I wish young pastors were treated with the same consideration as pastors with more experience. I am afraid, however, that as long as churches feel the desperate need to fill a ministerial vacancy, some will continue to abuse the vocational vulnerabilities of younger clergy in order to get a warm body in the pastor's office. My prayer is that denominations, seminaries, and other ministries will work towards educating congregations on the value of a prayerful, patient, and honest search process, and that more congregations will come to see the value in young clergy rather than simply viewing us as a cheap and easy alternative.

CHRIS THOMAS is the Pastor of the First Baptist Church of Williams in Jacksonville, Alabama. He holds the MDiv from George W. Truett Theological Seminary at Baylor University and a BA in Religion from Samford University. He enjoys traveling with his wife, reading Southern fiction (especially Flannery O'Connor), studying history and current homiletical trends, and walking alongside others on the shared journey of faith.

8

Dumbfounded: Thoughts on Resurrection Power, Human Finitude, and the Good Samaritan for Young Pastors Burning Out

A.J. Swoboda

The original text of Mark's short Gospel ends abruptly with a few women who'd followed Jesus running and screaming—"dumbfounded" (Gr. *exethambethesan*)—away from the empty tomb on Easter day (Mark 16:8). It's widely accepted by biblical scholarship that some later redactor/s (possibly even Mark himself) felt it necessary to splice a director's cut ending into the narrative in order to smooth out the rough transition of the awkward Easter finale. The most likely reason being it was too scandalous for the early church that Jesus would have revealed himself as resurrected Lord first and foremost to a bunch of women and *not* the disciples. All said and done, I appreciate the original ending most. It draws me in and makes more sense to me. Sure, the alternative ending is fine and canonical. It's just that the original, more abrupt ending is a bit more faithful to the Easter story, both ancient and contemporary. Specifically, that is, for young pastors who are experiencing real burnout.

My first Easter as a pastor was overwhelming if not ungodly. I found myself running away from the empty tomb "dumbfounded." What was most surprising about my first Easter as the pastor of a local church was how much work it required and the level of stress it created. Resurrection was alarmingly bad for my blood pressure. This, of course, wasn't news to those who have been in the business for some time. Holy week—as often quoted from the annals of pastoral oral tradition—is quite simply a week of hell for clergy. There is tremendous truth to this, I've discovered. Holy

Week can kill a pastor. One might surmise, as I had previously, that with the freshness of the empty tomb, the bright joy of forgiveness upon the garden's flowers just above it, and the everlasting life promised from the angel in white, Easter would bring us a week of celebration, rest, and good food. I was deceived. Resurrection requires way more administrative work than I'd ever have imagined. Christians get antsy. People are grumpier. Tithes are down. And the kids are always a bit more on edge than normal.

The stress clergy put on themselves at Easter is almost incomparable to any other point in the liturgical year. And it should be, considering that every member of our communities will be dragging their non-Christian friends to church by sheer force the one day a year they'll even toy with the idea. No stress, right? Just possibly the only chance they'll have to hear the good news of Jesus all year long. Easy peasy, right? It wouldn't surprise me in the least to discover that pastoral heart attacks and drug overdoses spike during Holy Week the same way they do (factually) on Monday mornings. Is there really something about the resurrected Lord that clogs arteries? Or is it that our religious systems are too hard for our hearts to handle? Either way, in the stress of Holy Week, we put on the best performance possible. Donning our skinny pants of eloquence, our high-*heals* of piety, and the lipstick of comedy, we do whatever we can to compel visitors to join our churches. But—and we all secretly know this—*it doesn't work*. We aren't good enough. And entertainment is a poor substitute for actual resurrection faith.

This whole stress-around-Easter thing isn't new. It's actually rather biblical. Consider how much *running around* there is in the Bible's Easter stories. Historically, the ancients were critical of running in public. Aristotle, it's believed, once said that it was never good for a "great-souled" (*megalapsychos*) person to run in public. It was embarrassing, he believed. It looked funny and implied that someone was not where he or she was supposed to be. It shouldn't go unnoticed to the biblical reader that Easter, and other pastoral regularities, indeed brings about a kind of *running around* in Scripture. There are few references to running in the New Testament. Almost all of them in the New Testament take place on or just around Easter. Just two days prior to Jesus' death, a naked man—purported to be Mark—flees during Jesus' arrest (Mark 14:51-52). Peter, the New Testament tells us, "ran to the tomb" in order to find Jesus (John 20:4). In comparing Mark's account with John's account of Easter, we find a bit of competition as well. John writes that he, "the one whom Jesus loves," got to the tomb before Peter, whose story is compiled in Mark's Gospel. One of the only other references to running in the New Testament writings is the Father "running" to his son in the parable of the prodigal (Luke 15:11-32). Running and Easter seemed to go hand in hand then, and they still do today.

In the quiet moments following Holy Week, I reflect. I usually realize I've missed something in the clamor of Easter: Easter often ceases, in those fleeting moments of pastoral entertainment, to be about celebrating the resurrected Lord. It functionally becomes a marketing opportunity to give the best spiritual performance of the year to get people to commit to my church and make my flock happy. But it doesn't work. Because the week after Easter, the flock is back to their normal selves, Easter Christians are back to not going to church, and I'm as tired as ever. And, frankly, thank God it doesn't work. Because if I have to give the performance of a lifetime to get people to come to church, then I'll have to give increasingly better performances to keep them coming back. If resurrection doesn't compel people, then trust me, your ability to entertain won't fill the void. Resurrection is the only thing that works on Easter. And there is nothing biblical about people being *entertained* by Easter. Again, originally, they ran away screaming.

This is the story of pastoral burnout: good-hearted people who want to help others get to the empty tomb, and save their health and integrity along the way, but have no idea how to do it. So we just run around a lot. How we do Easter is paradigmatic of most pastoral burnout; we secretly believe and practice that the best homage to Christ's resurrection life is paid by working ourselves to death. I think there is a way to overcome this.

Because so much of the American church lacks a unifying governing body or a Pope, it has to follow something. Often, especially for Evangelicals, this turns out to be conferences and publications. Evangelical orthodoxy is almost entirely mediated through books and big gatherings of pastors. Because of this, the lack of small church pastors that are celebrated in American Christianity is disconcerting. Few books are written on the heroes of churches of fifty. Our heroes are the big churches. This discrepancy is important, because we all shape our ministry on *some* hero. Pastors, above all, revere their heroes. Following these heroes brings a whole set of assumptions, some good and some atrocious. The pastoral heroes of my tradition are all individuals who gave themselves so wholeheartedly, so relentlessly, so passionately that they all burned out at one point or another. Many of these heroes are pastors of very large churches who wield great influence and power and are respected. In a way, I've been handed a theology that celebrates pastoral burnout.[23] Certainly, part of this is the zeal that comes with Pentecostal theology and the desire to help people experience the grace of faith. I have held tightly to A. W. Tozer's saying that we should always beware of any minister who does not have a limp. I think that's true. In order to connect with the harsh realities of life that parishioners deal with, it is ideal for pastors to have endured some of their own bumps and bruises too, which have led them to cling to God intensely. But should it be assumed that if a pastor is healthy, he or she shouldn't be trusted?

Can we truly preach about a resurrection life if it isn't one we are experiencing ourselves? Burnout is not the resurrection life. It is not the "abundant life" Jesus promised (John 10:10). In fact, I would go so far as to suggest that burning out is a great stumbling block to people hearing the gospel come out of our mouths. Our lives that lead to burnout eventually turn our theology of restoration and healing into complete hypocrisy to a watching world.[24] So we have to start questioning our heroes and what they taught us. Not rejecting them but questioning them. As my grandpa would put it, "Eat the meat, spit out the bone." Find the good and relentlessly question the unhealthy.

I want to suggest two ways I've learned to embrace life-giving, resurrection-power fulfillment in my crazy pastoral existence. First, I've begun to reject the notion of *pastoral martyrdom* that I've seen so often praised in our conferences and writings. I do this by practicing self-care. We must critique any theological or practical paradigm we have been handed that tells us we are the solution to God's problems in the world. Immediately, we are faced with a practical issue. One of the single greatest challenges for a pastor of a local church is the stark reality that the work of pastoral care is never finished. The lost will always need evangelizing, the Christians will perpetually need discipling, and the council will endlessly need meetings. Ministry fills up your to-do list rather quickly.

Why? I guess the immediate answer is that the kingdom of God has a lot of *coming* to do. Jesus, on the cross at Calvary, uttered, "It is finished." Only Jesus has biblical permission to utter such language over the work of saving the world; pastors do not. Early on in their ministries, pastors can easily overextend themselves, work eighty hours a week, and give every living breath of energy to the discipleship of people in their communi-ties. As time progresses, however, it becomes more and more challenging to live out such unsustainable practices. Get a spouse, a few children, a dog, a home to keep up, a hobby, and/or another job, and your calendar is overflowing. Statistically speaking, church plants either tend to grow and thrive after three years or they begin to die. While there are demographic, sociological, and perhaps even spiritual dimensions to this reality, I would suggest that the greatest reason for the eventual decline of a church planter is his or her unwillingness to incorporate sustainable, life-giving practices by the time the church has reached this age. Pastors need to learn how to care for themselves.

There are two conflicting reports about self-care in Scripture. On one hand, the Bible openly critiques spiritual leaders who care for themselves alone to the detriment of the care of others. The prophetic utterance of Ezekiel takes to task the shepherds of Israel who are self-focused, self-attentive, and self-helping:

> Woe to you shepherds of Israel who only take care of yourselves! Should not shepherds take care of the flock? You eat the curds, clothe yourselves with the wool and slaughter the choice animals, but you do not take care of the flock. You have not strengthened the weak or healed the sick or bound up the injured. You have not brought back the strays or searched for the lost. You have ruled them harshly and brutally. (Ezek 34:2-4)

Yet, in the incarnation, Jesus openly models self-care that complements the words of Ezekiel. Jesus, the Son of the Living God, fed himself, slept on a boat, went on long prayer walks, and ate with friends. We tend towards one or the other: complete care of others or complete neglect of others. If we gravitate only towards the care of others, we cease being pastors and become spiritual communists who have to be involved in everyone's life, every church activity, and every decision. This desire for totalitarianism will lead to death of the pastor (burnout or literal death). And this is a tendency for everyone in ministry. As Paul Tournier once wrote, the "germ of totalitarianism also lies dormant inside all of us."[25] Or we become entirely self-focused. When this happens, no one is being discipled, cared for, or led into kingdom living. The outcome of this will be the eventual death of the church. Both extremes, in the end, lead to the death of something.

There is a third way that brings life. What is often suggested at this point is *balance* between the two. But I believe the most helpful practice is not *balance* but *radical presence*. By this, I mean that a pastor must be faithful to mark out clear times, as appropriate, to care for others: praying, helping, discipling, and correcting. As well, the pastor must mark out clear times that he or she is off-limits to the body of the church for the purposes of being with family, self, and God. When we are faithful to do this, we will find ourselves ready for the task of caring for others. As John Piper wrote, "God is most glorified in us when we are most satisfied in him."[26]

So pastors must get a second life. In this life, which does not require ministry to be done, we can find a world of joy, fun, laughter, and community. Creativity is of the essence. I have personally developed a few life-giving activities that require nothing of me on a spiritual or leadership level. On my days off (Tuesdays and Wednesdays), I first devote an afternoon to gardening and to caring for the yard. While this kind of activity is *work* for some, it is *joy* and *play* for me. My son puts on his farmer overalls and gets into the dirt with his daddy. Second, I will take my wife out to dinner once a week. The key to this is not the place or the time. The key is my phone: *it must be off.* The phone, in our culture, is no longer a little plastic and metal device that allows us to call someone. The phone is now a portal into the world of work. When that phone is on, so am I. In fact, I found that my blood pressure decreases when my phone is off. Why? When it is on, the possibility for emergency and work is on. Not to mention when my phone is off, it disciples other people in my community to self-solve the problems of the church and the world. Third, I will sit down and read a book or my Bible for no purpose other than reading. Sadly, one of the casualties of pastoring and preaching is the loss of *devotional Scripture reading* that isn't being formed into three points for Sunday.

The self-care I describe here requires us to do both—care for self and care for others—with all of our hearts, at all moments. Strive for extremes, not necessarily balance. Do each wholeheartedly when you do them. I recall a dear pastor friend telling me once that it isn't my job to die for the church; he reminded me that somebody already did that. The church has already been bought at a great price on the wooden splinters of two nailed boards on a hill outside Jerusalem. Those whom God calls to care for his vineyard are a sad and pathetic substitution for the real thing.

Also, alongside self-care we must embrace a strong pastoral theology of human finitude. Whether we like it or not, God has canonized this into all of our pastoral ministries. Adam and Eve were never pre-packaged as needless, self-sufficient beings. They got hungry and lonely. Sin didn't help. So, in a way, all ministry must be conceived as being just a little east of Eden. We sometimes fail to recognize this by thinking our ministry is different, our church is special, and we are doing it uniquely. *We all think our ministry is squarely back in Eden.* Everyone else has been cast out. This is hubris of the first degree. Embracing pastoral finitude shifts our thinking. It is when we believe in our pastoral perfection and omnipresence that we will meet burnout around the corner. Embracing our finitude helps us avoid it. No longer must people stay at my church in order to be called Christians. I can now imagine my church as a rest stop where some people may come, drop off some of their spiritual baggage, hear a good message, be refreshed, and leave on the highway of life never to be seen again. Spiritual tourists aren't bad; rather, they are people from another land where Jesus is working too.

I realize this may sound a bit gnostic or brain-centered. I'll warn you, however, that this is not some esoteric mind game. Scripture knows what it is talking about: "As a person *thinks* in their heart, so they are" (Prov 23:7). Over time, our lives become our theologies. By believing more strongly in our inability to be, do, and enact everything under the sun, we give Jesus permission to be Lord in our lives. We all, at times, forget our imperfect and broken nature. We also forget how we see things from a very different angle than God does. Broadly, the two most dangerous pastoral sins are making mountains out of molehills and making molehills out of mountains. We emphasize the small stuff and underplay the big stuff. Burnout is the product of either side. As finite people, we can only see things from our tiny little perspective, which is almost always not the full picture. A finite pastor chooses to realize she or he *never* has the whole picture of anything. Our theology is always a little broken, our church is always a little broken, and our lives are always a little broken. Embracing this truth is freeing. It allows us to embody where real people in our churches are in their lives. It gives permission for all of us to be who we are.

This has come to me over and over in the parable of the good Samaritan (Luke 10:30-37). A man is on the side of the road nearly dead after being beaten and robbed on his way to Jericho from Jerusalem. Two religious people—a priest and a Jew—walk by and do nothing. After some time, another less pious individual takes note and stops to help. This one is a Samaritan, the dirtiest of half-Jews. The Samaritan takes the broken man to the local inn and pays for his care. The innkeeper is asked to look after the broken man until the Samaritan returns. And the story ends with Jesus' listeners pondering what they would have done. What if Jesus was the Samaritan? And the role of the follower of Christ was that of the innkeeper?

Pastors are the innkeepers, not the good Samaritans. We are temporal, short-term solutions. Our role is to care for the broken that Christ, the Samaritan, has brought to our place until he returns in glory. Then, when Christ steps in, we get out of the way. We should not forget that part of the pastoral call is surely the mundane role of running the inn, the church. But the other is *literally* taking care of those in the inn. We will face tensions in that calling. It is an odd and awkward role for an innkeeper to have to run a business, pay the bills, and keep the heat going, all while simultaneously offering love and charity to visitors in the inn. When we believe in our own "good Samaritan*ness*," we become the heroes in our own story. But we aren't the heroes. We should stop acting as such.

A. J. SWOBODA is the Pastor of Theophilus Church in urban Portland, Oregon, and directs Blessed Earth Northwest, an organization that helps Christians care for God's creation. He also teaches theology, biblical studies, and Christian history at George Fox Evangelical Seminary and Fuller Theological Seminary. He holds the PhD in Theology from the University of Birmingham (UK), the MA in Theological Studies from George Fox Evangelical Seminary, and a BA in Pastoral Studies and Greek from Eugene Bible College. He is the author of a number of books, including *Tongues and Trees: Towards a Pentecostal Ecological Theology* (Deo, 2013), *Introducing Evangelical Ecotheology* (Baker Academic, 2014), and *A Glorious Dark* (Baker, 2015). Follow him at www.ajswoboda.com.

9

Finding the Grace: The Life and Times of a Young Priest

Jeremiah Williamson

I guess I realized that my young age would occasionally be a vocational stumbling block for others during seminary. I started just after turning twenty-two, and I went with the intention of eventually earning a doctorate in hopes of becoming a religion professor at a small liberal arts college. But in my first year of seminary, I felt the call to ordained ministry in the Episcopal Church.

No ordination process is easy, nor should it be. I experienced much grace in the process, encountering amazing people who affirmed my calling and my gifts. And while, thankfully, I came through with fewer scars than some of my friends, the process did prepare me, perhaps unintentionally, for the age discrimination that would sometimes arise in my ordained ministry.

My last step before ordination was Candidacy. I knew once I was made a Candidate, I could begin planning my first ordination—to the transitional diaconate. After my day of interviews with the Commission on Ministry, I was informed that I had been approved, though there were some concerns. I would be given the details during my meeting with the chair of the commission. I chose, at the time, to rejoice in the good news, even if my mind was obsessing over what was to come.

It turns out that the "concerns" were just my age. That was made clear during my follow-up meeting. The commission chair invited me into her office and congratulated me on being made a Candidate, although it was important to her that I not get too excited. The commission did have concerns, after all. She went on to explain, "See, we have to overlook a lot with you young candidates. There is a lot of immaturity. We think you will be a good priest, but you still have some growing up to do. You need more life experience." I was about to get married, and she knew I was moving to Ohio because my wife had an appointment in a United Methodist Church in the Youngstown, Ohio, area set to begin a few months later. And so she advised me, "Move with your wife to Ohio. Get yourself a job working at a shoe store or something. Maybe find a local church and just offer to help out some. Get some life experience and then, in a couple of years, you will be ordained."

Thankfully, the good people of the Diocese of Ohio, including Bishop Mark Hollingsworth, recognized my gifts for ordained ministry. They saw that I was, despite my age—or maybe even because of my age—an asset, so I was ordained just months after my conversation with the chair of the Commission on Ministry.

My first ordained position was as the Assistant Rector of St. John's Episcopal Church in Youngstown, Ohio, one of those cities that rose and fell on the back of the steel industry. And while I believe it is rising from the ashes of its terrible hardships, there is still plenty of poverty there.

Like in many industrial cities, the downtown area has suffered greatly from decades of economic struggle. St. John's was one of the few churches to stick it out downtown. Because of our location and reputation as a generous congregation, it was not uncommon for folks to wander into the nave on a Sunday morning in search of food or financial assistance.

Being an Assistant Rector meant I was blessed to work closely with a more experienced colleague. The Rector with whom I served was a large Southern man named John. In his sixties and having been ordained for three decades, John is the kind of man who has the size to physically move people into place but also the gentle kindness that makes the repositioning feel benevolent. He had been at St. John's about seven years when I arrived.

One week he was on vacation and I was leading the Sunday services. During coffee hour after worship, in the rear of the nave by the front entrance, I was approached by one of the members. He came over with a woman who had popped in that Sunday morning looking for cash, I think, to help her get to a town in which she had family. Maybe she needed money for gas or bus fare; I can no longer remember. I do remember her reaction to me, however. I must have been twenty-six or twenty-seven years old at the time. She approached me and said disappointedly, "I was hoping to talk to a real priest. Is there a real priest here?"

In the life of a young priest, it seems that the negative age-related comments almost always occur in the absence of relationship. Once the congregation knows me, as people experience my hard work and love for them, age is no longer an issue. But until that relationship is established, it is not uncommon for folks to work from preconceptions and prejudices.

I was a twenty-eight-year-old priest with two and a half years of parish-based, ordained ministry experience under my cincture when I decided to look for a Rector position. The first parish to which I applied sent me back a letter indicating they were looking for someone with more "experience." Though I was concerned that this response might be frustratingly familiar, it was actually the one and only time that happened. Every parish that granted me a phone interview made me a finalist in their search process.

That, of course, includes St. Andrew's Episcopal Church in Toledo, Ohio, where I currently serve. And while most of the search committee considered my relatively young age to be a positive trait, there was one exception. Two weeks after I began, I heard from a parish leader that one of the search committee members was planning to leave the parish because of me. I called him, half convinced that we could talk things out. Perhaps that was a naïve notion, though I prefer to say it was hopeful. He informed me that, while everyone else "drank the Kool-Aid," he was the lone voice of opposition to the committee's selection. He, of the Baby Boom generation, said I was too young to be his priest, too young to be a Rector. "I would actually rather have a woman priest than you," he said to me in a statement that was meant to offend me on multiple levels; my wife is ordained in the United Methodist Church. This man stayed for another year; he poked at me on and off during that time—sometimes playfully, sometimes not. After years of burning bridges within the parish, he finally decided to go elsewhere. In what I know was meant to be a compliment, even though it will sound under-handed to an outsider, the last thing he said to me, after the Great Vigil of Easter was, "You know, I must admit, you have come a long way in a year."

Most often the age discrimination is subtler, often accidental, and really one of the lesser headaches in the life of a parish priest. More often I am surprised by grace. There was another member of the search committee named Chuck. In his nineties, he is the oldest member of my congregation and has been in the parish since his youth. While looking through the stack of clergy profiles, before the interviews and meetings, Chuck, I am told, pulled my file and announced to the committee, "This is the one." I was twenty-eight at the time.

After I accepted the call, but before I arrived, the search committee informed the congregation of their choice. The chair of the committee was nervous to announce that they had selected a twenty-something priest to follow my retired predecessor. But Chuck was not nervous. He stood before the congregation and simply said, "If I don't have a problem with his age, neither should you." I have now served with the people of St. Andrew's for four years.

There are challenges that come with being young in one's vocation, no doubt about it. I have few colleagues who are my contemporaries. In my diocese, we are closing more parishes than we are opening—a strange environment in which to start a vocation that I intend to hold for forty years. Weddings and funerals still tend to evoke many age-related comments, even though I am now thirty-two. Of course they are usually attached to a compliment: "That was a great service, Father. You look really young. How old are you?"

But mostly I have found that as the church is changing and being changed, what is at one level painful for many, even scary, is also opening hearts. Eyes are being opened to the many and diverse individuals through whom the Holy Spirit is working. This parish, St. Andrew's, embraced me. They have embraced my spouse. And when we had a baby, the first time in the parish's history that the Rector had a baby while serving the parish, they celebrated with us; they threw us a baby shower, and members of the parish continue to sit with our son during worship.

Despite the challenges, I am confident that I will one day look back and miss my years as a young priest. I will look back, remembering the challenges but seeing the grace.

JEREMIAH WILLIAMSON is the Rector of St. Andrew's Episcopal Church in Toledo, Ohio. He previously served as the Curate of St. John's Episcopal Church in Youngstown, Ohio. He holds the MDiv from Drew Theological School, Diploma in Anglican Studies from the General Theological Seminary, and BA in Contemporary Music from Greenville College. He enjoys spending time with his wife, Jennifer, a United Methodist pastor, and their adorable sons. His first book, *Praying the Scriptures*, was released in 2014 by Church Publishing. Follow him at www.jeremiahwilliamson.blogspot.com.

10

When Grief Is Good and Grace Is Great

Matthew L. Richard

Early Observations

A few years after I walked forward in an evangelistic youth meeting in Belmont, Texas, I began seeing signs that church life was not as full of "roses and rainbows" as I thought. Brother Bob,[27] the name by which we called our beloved leader and shepherd at Friendship Baptist Church, shared during service one Sunday that he was taking a leave of absence. Friendship was a typical "rank and file" Southern Baptist Church (SBC). From the Lottie Moon Christmas Offering to spring revival to checking off weekly duties on the offering envelopes, we did it all in lock step. True to form, the church began years ago as a split from another prominent congregation in town, when mischief arose involving the pastor and the secretary. Those who have been in ministry for a long while might read all this and think, "How more cliché can you get?" However, it did not seem cliché to me. A few years after walking forward in front of thousands of people and "asking Jesus to come into my heart," I began considering what a vocational ministry might look like. So if my pastor at Friendship Baptist needed to take some unscheduled time off, I wanted to know why. I asked Sunday school teachers, deacons, and youth group friends, but no one gave me a straight answer.

Thankfully, Brother Bob eventually returned and my concerns faded—at least for about a year. Then there was turmoil all over again when he quit for good, this time citing that God had "laid this decision on his heart." One of the first memories I have of a Baptist business meeting involved voting whether or not to grant him a severance package. After hearing a faction of men who were against doing so stand up and speak, pointing to Brother Bob's "liberal leanings" and his penchant for getting too many ideas from the Internet (this occurred in the late 1990s) as their supporting reasons, I began to understand why he needed that leave of absence a year ago. It did not seem to matter to this group that the church had the most people in attendance in their history under Brother Bob's leadership, or that he had successfully led them through a building campaign that enlarged their educational facilities. He was now their enemy, and it seemed to me, in their thinking, he would now pay the consequences. I promised myself that I would *not* let this happen to me. I did not know what Brother Bob did wrong to land on their bad side, and I'm not entirely sure he knew either. In spite of this conflict and its unresolved nature, though, I became even more determined to pursue a vocation in ministry.

Where It All Began

My first permanent position was that of associate pastor at Hopeful Baptist Church in Hankins, Texas, a congregation of twenty to thirty people that began as a mission of a bigger Baptist church in town. Over time it had become autonomous, but had not increased much from the original group that started it in the 1980s. My position was created because the elderly pastor was not ready to retire, but also did not want to preach every Sunday. The person who had it before me was a close friend who had moved on and "gotten his own church," as we sometimes say. So this seemed like a perfect position for a young, starry-eyed preacher to have in college, the kind that allowed me to preach without having the full responsibilities of running a church.

For the first few months, things were great. The little church took my fiancée and me in as their own. They gave us lots of warm hugs, good food, and sincere friendship. We helped them start a Sunday school class for children and filled the baptistery for the first time in a long while. It was fun all around, except for one man whom I sensed did not like me. Rob Sawyer, the church's treasurer and sole Sunday school teacher, went out of his way *not* to shake my hand on Sunday mornings. When I brought this up to my fiancée, she told me I was probably imagining it. I never confronted him. Instead, being a stubborn college student, I forced him to shake my hand as often as possible, while he would look past me and refuse eye contact.

When Hopeful's pastor decided to step down permanently, I was the obvious choice for successor. I was nominated and my candidacy scheduled to be voted on on the pastor's last Sunday. The joyful anticipation that filled the morning was deceptive, however. I assumed that the large crowd assembled, many whom were not regulars, and some whom I had never met, were there because of excitement surrounding the possibly of getting a new, young pastor. When asked to leave at the end of the service before the voting started, as is customary Baptist polity, I had no doubt that it was simply a formality. I was wrong.

As it turned out, Rob not only disliked me but had also shared his low opinion of me following the meeting in which I was nominated to be the next pastor. "If he is the next pastor, I'm leaving," he told the group. Unbeknownst to me and others, the large crowd present when I preached was not there to cheer for me. They were there to defend Rob. They consisted of his family, in-laws, and friends—all who somehow happened to be church members. Their votes had just enough pull to drop the number of affirming votes right under 75 percent, which is what the church's bylaws stated was the minimum percentage necessary to call a pastor.

I couldn't believe it. This was a horrible way to start out in ministry. At least Brother Bob helped Friendship build a building before he left. I was not given a chance to build anything. Perhaps the dagger that most wounded my heart, however, was simply the unknown about what I had done to receive this level of opposition. No one could tell me why Rob had issues with me. In retrospect, he probably did not know either. In the moment, I took refuge in Jesus' promise that I am indeed "blessed . . . when people insult [me], persecute [me] and falsely say all kinds of evil against [me] because of [him]."[28]

I've since succumbed to reality. Rob did not begrudge me on account of Jesus. Brother Bob's detractors did not pressure him because of a particular theological opinion. Sometimes personalities clash in church. The more autonomous the church, the greater the possibility for conflict. In the midst of facing such repercussions at Hopeful, I missed out on an important element. The church knew that Rob did not like me, but they nominated me anyway. If he had followed through with his threat to leave, the church would not only have lost a Sunday school teacher, treasurer, and deacon; they would also have lost one of their biggest financial contributors.

Over 70 percent of the church was willing to put these assets on the line to gain a nineteen-year-old college student as their pastor. What a powerful affirmation! When received appropriately, affirmations like this can significantly motivate one in ministry. Following Brother Bob's resignation, his office door was completely covered with butcher paper. On it numerous members of the congregation wrote verses of Scripture and notes of encouragement. Piles of cards were taped to it and left at the foot of the entryway. This proved to be a prevailing sight, and perhaps had a hand in spurring me toward a pastoral vocation that would inevitably include pain and loss.

Too Good to Be True

As if in apology for my previous experience, my next place of service proved to be a delight. At this point, my fiancée and I had married and moved to central Texas, and I had begun attending seminary. In addition to my full-time coursework, I longed to have an outlet to express all that I was learning, which is where Sandy Creek Baptist Church came in. It was similar to Hopeful in some ways. It was small, in the middle of nowhere, and required a minimal amount of time from my schedule. I heard about the opening from their previous pastor, who was transitioning following his upcoming seminary graduation. It was as simple as calling the church and expressing my interest. The next thing I knew, I was driving an hour into rural ranching country for consideration to be their next pastor.

The element that made Sandy Creek a joy was that the congregation had decided that part of their mission was to train young pastors. They were well in touch with reality and understood that I was only going to be there for a few years. In hindsight, those years went by way too fast. Sandy Creek became a second family to us. I still remember the sign-up sheet they had on the bulletin board to provide meals for us, the monthly potlucks that were looked forward to with excitement, and the joy they expressed when we simply spent the day with them in their homes. Sandy Creek's lone Sunday school teacher was also a man of influence, but he was the antithesis of Rob. On more than one occasion he told me that I would never be able to forget Spring Creek, and he was right.

The Real World

Nevertheless, Sandy Creek was not the real world. Most churches do not believe it is primarily their job to minister to the pastor. The real world, it turned out, was not very far from where we lived when I attended seminary. Ben Dobbs, then pastor of one of the most prestigious and largest Baptist churches in central Texas, was my mentor. He knew of a church he'd pastored previously that was looking for its next leader. He offered the search committee a glowing recommendation of me, and I am convinced that this was the sole contributing factor for me being called to my current place of service. I've been here for two and a half years, and every day is a new challenge. One hundred and twenty people on a Sunday morning may not sound like much, but it is a huge leap from twenty. Before I interviewed with the search committee, Ben assured me, "I would never recommend you to a church that I thought to be in a difficult situation," and I believed him. He arranged for the search committee to come and hear me preach during an evening service at his church, and afterwards my wife and I met with them at a nearby Mexican restaurant.

I was impressed by several things about the committee: the number of young people, the diversity in gender, and their honesty. They were upfront about some present conflict among the church staff, but they expressed confidence that all the church needed was a "good leader." I do not think the church intended to mislead us, but it did. The committee was brimming with some of the church's youngest and brightest people, but the actual church involvement of individual members varied significantly. Today, two of the members no longer attend, two others are "pew-sitters," and the remaining three are fairly faithful. I thought you had to be a committed church member to serve on a search committee, but that was not the case with them.

Maybe I was too anxious to get a full-time church, or a bit naïve regarding what kinds of problems to expect, but the responsibility I found myself holding hit me like a ton of bricks my first week at the office. The staff problems I'd heard about got louder and louder as others stopped by to give me their take on the situation. I greatly appreciated our treasurer, who overheard bits and pieces of each person's opinion and volunteered to lay everything out objectively when I asked what she thought. The problems would be nothing new to anyone who has studied church conflict: the youth and music ministers didn't like the children's minister, the children's minister felt underappreciated, and all of them had threatened to quit at one point or another. Part of me wanted to let all of them quit, until I learned that each one had a "following" in the congregation. I could not be the pastor who ran off someone who had been at the church for twenty years when I hadn't been there for twenty days!

This became my main concern. A crisis was looming, and I needed to be the proactive pastor who would quiet the storm. So, thinking myself to be wise, I arranged individual meetings with all three staff members. In each of those, I was told just how dedicated that staff member was and how undervalued his or her efforts were, especially in the cases of the youth and children's ministers. If these two were going to work together, something needed to be done, and everyone seemed to be telling me that I was the person to do it. I had no idea how hopeless the cause was when I set up a joint meeting for the three of us to sit down and talk through the issues.

I'm not educated in the field of psychology, but I've watched enough episodes of *Dr. Phil* to know that you are not supposed to use phrases like "always" and "never" when referring to what you do not like about another person. When I asked where they thought the conflict originated, this was exactly the direction the conversation went. I tried my best to be an active listener by spouting off phrases like, "So what I hear you saying is . . . ," and "Say more about that." This only seemed to make the problem worse, and the meeting ended with both of them storming out of my office and me feeling like I had failed to be the leader I wanted to be.

My emotions ran the gambit: fear, anger, confusion, frustration, and even resignation. I had never handled anything like this in my life. Part of me wondered, "Do these people have any idea that I am just a kid with barely any life experience?" The only thing I had learned in my previous church was how to preach, eat, and visit sick people. I felt that this church should have thought twice before scooping up a young minister and ruining his first post-seminary experience. Since then, people have asked, "Has the honeymoon worn off yet?" To which I respond, "There never was a honeymoon!" I spent a lot of time praying, crying, and doubting that first week. Then, it happened: the youth minister resigned.

I waited for the backlash: the angry phone calls, threatening e-mails, and hallway confrontations where I was raked over the coals for allowing this beloved youth minister to leave. Strangely, none of that happened. Sure, people have grumbled here and there, and blame has been assigned by some, but not to me. It sounds trite, but distance and time are often the best elements for a fresh perspective. I'm not sure I could have done anything different to change the outcome, or, if I had done something else, that another person would not have resigned. I do know that this was a difficult way to begin my ministry here. I still do not know why the mismatched committee told me that the church just needed a "good leader," or why they thought that this person might be me. I do not know what the staff expected me or any new pastor to do about the issues they had with one another, or why they thought it was acceptable to fight in front of someone who was young enough to be their child.

What I do know is that I am still here, and I have not destroyed the church! I've heard it simplistically stated that "God does not call the equipped, but he equips the called." I often do not feel equipped, and on my worst days I am not too sure what "being called" is all about. However, not every day is my worst day. My first week on the job still rates as some of the toughest days I have ever experienced in church. I stayed bitter and angry about that for a while, but maybe it's time to see it as an avenue to becoming more equipped. For this early part of ministry, I've leaned on Scripture's promise that Christ's "grace is sufficient for [*me,*] for [*his*] power is made perfect in weakness."[29] I am still thankful for this wonderful truth, but could it be that I am a little stronger than I thought?

MATTHEW L. RICHARD is the Pastor of a Baptist church in Central Texas. He holds the MDiv from George W. Truett Theological Seminary at Baylor University and a BA in Religion from East Texas Baptist University. With a passion for preaching, reading, and writing, he is blessed to have a wonderful wife, a sweet daughter, and a goofy dog. Follow him at http://boastinginweaknessblog.blogspot.com.

11

When Two Are Called: A Life of Ministry as a Husband and Wife Clergy Team

Brian & Kimberly Miller

"You both were meant for us" was the comment that struck us during the ordination council. It had been a long road, full of discouraging and confusing twists and turns. The statement was made by a prominent church member and well-respected deacon. It was the kind of affirmation we had longed for.

Kim's Call

The statement "You both were meant for us" implied a kind of affirmation I believed I could never receive. Growing up in a small, conservative Southern Baptist Church, I had been taught that preaching, ordination, and pastoring were out of the question for me. It was an absolute truth in Baptist life that men were to be the leaders and women were limited to children's ministry, missions, and speaking at women-only events. So naturally I was confused when, during a Sunday evening service, I clearly heard God speak to me. He called me to surrender my life to ministry. At first I told no one, believing it must be a mistake. When the feeling did not go away, I convinced myself it must be a call to missions. I became vocal about telling people that I was going to become a medical missionary, an acceptable and noble calling even for a woman. But deep down, buried so deep that I refused for a long time even to acknowledge it, I knew what I was really called to do. I was called to preach. It was a desire that came from God alone. I wanted more than anything to be a pastor. I could not tell anyone because my news would only have been met with a chorus of "You can't do that. You heard from God wrong. God does not call women."

Brian's Call

I had always loved church and dreamed of doing what the "men in coats" did. As a child, I told everyone that Jesus loves them, and so my call into ministry as a young teenager was not a surprise. I was the fourth young man from my church to be called into ministry in as many years. I became the "poster child" for the church youth group, even though I did not always feel this was a positive thing. I put unfair expectations on myself and often felt ashamed when I did not live up to them. I was warned that ministry would be difficult, but no one took the time to tell me about the real challenges. Even though I had the support of the whole congregation, I lacked a mentor to offer true guidance and transparency about a ministerial calling. In June 2000, I was on my way to the Southern Baptist Convention in Orlando, Florida, with only a vague idea of what would happen there. Growing up, I only experienced one way to "do church" and always looked to others for biblical and spiritual answers. During the gathering, a motion was brought to the floor to limit the position of "pastor" to men. Along with a little over half of the people there, I raised my ballot in the air to affirm that motion. Shortly after the convention, I left for college.

The Beginning of Our Journey (Brian)

In August 2000, we found ourselves at the Baptist College of Florida in Graceville. Through the difficult circumstance of losing her sister Angel, Kim had given up on becoming a doctor. The trauma of Angel's death sent Kim's life and family into a tailspin. She realized medical school was out of the question for many reasons, including finances and lack of support from family due to the extreme grief. So she reexamined her calling and turned her attention to becoming a teacher and children's minister. I found myself matriculating at the college for a different reason. I had been encouraged by my pastor and knew that two other young men from my church had chosen to pursue their degrees there.

Kim and I each moved into our dorms, and we met on the second day of orientation. Our time in college was formative. One professor, Dr. Jack Cunningham, encouraged all of his students, male and female, to remember that it does not matter what title the church gives you because it is God who calls us "ministers." That professor was influential and a blessing to us both. The other significant influence was our pastors. Pastors Tommy and Donna were the first ministry couple we'd ever known. He served as pastor and she as minister of music and education. Given how the church looked up to and supported them both as ministers, we knew this was a model that was actually possible as we began to dream about what life and ministry together would look like.

While this was the example we saw at church, a very different example was prominent on campus. Many married couples with children lived in campus housing. In most of these cases, only the husband was a student, or at least only he was encouraged to finish his degree. Wives homeschooled children and husbands worked, went to school, and served as ministers. We often found ourselves struggling in our efforts to fit these conflicting expectations of a "complementary relationship" with our particular dreams and callings. The effort frequently resulted in arguments and feelings of defeat, inadequacy, and shame. While both of us knew that God had called us to serve together, I struggled with knowing what roles were acceptable for women, and Kim struggled to vocalize what she truly felt called to do.

Our First Church (Kim)

Toward the end of our last semester in college, Brian was called to his first pastorate in southwest Georgia. On the same day he preached in view of the call, he was also being voted on. While he was preparing to accept the call, I was belittled by the chairman of deacon's wife for not putting shoes on our young, non-walking daughter. The necessity of accepting the call to meet our financial needs was counterintuitive. Our gut instincts said, "This is not a good fit." After speaking to the previous pastor, who was a friend and fellow student, we were assured that "the church would love us." However, the excitement of finally having a ministry was overshadowed by the insecurities that developed in our marriage because of the way the church treated us, especially me.

A couple of months after moving in, I gave birth to a son. Not a single person from the church called, came over, or made a meal. It felt like hell. We never felt loved. We never felt respected or wanted. At one point a church member told us that the church was going to die. When we asked what the church was willing to do about it, the response was, "Let it die." We found ourselves trying to implement all of the things we had been taught about how to grow a church, but we were faced with a church that did not want to grow. We were faced with a church that was resigned to death. There was nothing we could do about it, and we were unprepared for that kind of scenario. In addition, we were unprepared for the loneliness of serving in a church that did not want us. We admittedly made many mistakes along the way, but there was no room for grace, especially for us as a young pastor and his family.

This was certainly not the ministry we had in mind. Brian was able to lead several in the community to Christ, but because they were African American, they were not "welcome in our church." This sentiment was expressed by the man who served as the chairman of deacons, youth director, treasurer, and mayor of the town! He or his wife was on every committee in the church. A secret deacons' meeting led to Brian being asked to resign.

After leaving this small church, we were allowed to move temporarily into the parsonage of a larger church, and Brian's résumé was sent across the state. We believed, however, that we would not need to search for long, as the church that had graciously given us housing also needed an Associate Pastor. Come to find out, though, the Director of Missions for our association also had plans for us. He attempted to force positions on us, and we later learned that he gave poor recommendations to other churches.

From Southeastern to CUDS (Brian)

We did not find a new position in Georgia, and, though it was never explicitly stated, Kim believed it was her fault. I struggled with my calling and began to believe that God was punishing me for seeking a church where we could both serve. It also took a toll on our marriage when Kim found out she was once again pregnant. We felt that our only option was to continue our education in hopes that having a Master of Divinity under our belts would open new doors. We moved onto the campus of an SBC seminary where our closest college friends already attended, only to have another door slammed in our face. "Our wives don't get MDivs," we were told as we sat in the admissions office. "If they receive a degree, it is a Master of Arts in Christian Education." I wanted to punch the wall on the way out. Again, we felt defeated. Pregnant with our third child and still experiencing postpartum depression after our second, Kim fell into an even deeper depression. We drifted further apart.

As God would have it, there was a silver lining. The same pastor who had offered us our first glimpse of ministry together was now leading a church in the seminary town. He pointed us to Campbell University Divinity School, about an hour away. Although initially we were too deep in our pain to see clearly, we would both become students there, and it would transform our lives, beliefs, and ministry. The journey to Campbell was not easy, though. Kim continued to struggle with depression.

In addition, as a newborn our precious daughter was hospitalized for an infection. This was emotionally difficult and financially devastating. We had little choice but to move in with family. When another traumatic event forced us to move once again, we became practically homeless.

We finally made the decision to attend Campbell entirely on faith. We had nothing else going for us. Our family and friends refused to support us, not fully understanding why we were still so committed to our call to ministry. Much like the prophet Jeremiah, ministry was a fire caught up in our bones. We could not go on, but we could not give up. The divinity school opened a whole new way to us. For Kim, it reawakened a long-abandoned dream of preaching. For me, getting to know women whose ministry included time in the pulpit, in addition to studying the history that led to the vote in 2000, gave me new understanding that changed my opinion.

Campbell became a place of healing. For one thing, we had stability. We had moved so many times that we were exhausted. For the five years in Buies Creek, we lived in the same apartment. God brought people to minister to us. A local association not only helped us move but also provided everything for our first Christmas there. We found a renewed respect for one another as ministers. We had opportunities to grow our ministry skills, and we learned to see and appreciate the ways we complemented one another. We were also humbled by our time in Buies Creek. We came to the place of realizing that our marriage needed major work. Thankfully, we found a good pastoral counselor who helped us revitalize our marriage and deal with individual hurts.

From "Recanting the Baptist Faith and Message" (Brian)

At the end of our divinity school journey and just before Kim's ordination, I was asked to write a blog that gave some insight into the change in our beliefs and thinking:

> Even during my seminary days . . . women pastors and the ordination of women were foreign to me. After several of my ministry friends—who happened to be women—were ordained, I became acquainted with the unfamiliar. As I began to appreciate and admire the giftedness and calling of these women, I began second-guessing my decisions and felt guilty over my vote in favor of the *Baptist Faith and Message* of 2000. Up to this point, I was trying to be the person that other people implied I ought to be rather than being who I was. I struggled with the question

of who I was to tell someone else, "No, God did not call you into ordained ministry because you are not the right gender." Yet that mindset was what my upbringing had taught me.[30]

I began giving myself permission to ask the difficult questions that my Southern Baptist roots had silenced. Does God really look at gender as a qualification for calling? Whose interpretation of the Bible do we follow? Can a woman be ordained if the church recognizes her calling into the ministry? As I struggled with these questions, God illuminated my heart. In the meantime, God was already working in Kim's heart. Within weeks of enrolling in a Christian history course titled "Women in the Christian Tradition," she opened up about her desire to preach.

Soon after, we began to explore the possibility of her ordination. We wanted to embrace it wholeheartedly, but our faith backgrounds hindered us. However, we were becoming more open to the idea. The next semester I took a Baptist history course with Dr. Lydia Hoyle. In that class, I read two books for a project that explored the two different sides of the division in the Southern Baptist Convention.

> I expected to see copyright dates on the books of 2002 or later. I was in disbelief to discover they were published in the 1990s. I soon discovered that the battle I was up against had been around longer than I have been alive. I came to terms with my understanding that the struggle was more about power than about doctrine. It was more about politics than religion and was more about interpretation than it was about the Bible. While studying the life and death of the third-century martyr Perpetua, I came to the conclusion that if a woman could give her life up *for* the faith then she could certainly give her life *to* the faith. I found myself desiring to send a pebble back to the SBC headquarters symbolizing the recantation of my vote in 2000. I have now come to the place in which I believe that any person should be able to pursue God's call on his or her life without someone else interpreting that call, whether it is in counseling, in the home, behind a desk, a lectern or even a pulpit.[31]

Continuing the Journey (Kim)

Even though we had come to this revelation, there were still struggles. The church we felt drawn to and began serving at the beginning of divinity school was conservative on their views of women in ministry, particularly in the pulpit. Yet we felt that God had called us to serve there nonetheless, and we were blessed to lead several successful ministries during our time. Our decision to stay served as a stumbling block for some churches with whom we interviewed. They said that if we believed differently than the church, we should not have stayed. We were convinced, however, that the gospel was more important than our opposing views. The church was doing good work and allowing us to use our gifts, talents, and experiences alongside them. At the same time, some churches we interviewed with said they had no problem with a female preacher/minister, but rejected the idea of a minister's wife having such a calling.

Finally, it seemed as though our prayers were being heard and God was about to pour out his blessing on us. We were in the interview process with a church that we believed was a perfect fit. Their previous pastor and his wife had served together, both allowed to preach and minister. The church was affiliated with all the "right" Baptist groups and seemed to have a vision compatible with our own. But alas, in God's providence, while we were becoming hopeful about that possibility, God opened the door to a small church in a rural town in North Carolina. Like us, the church had struggled with its identity as Baptists who affirmed women in ministry. When we interviewed, we were transparent, firm, and unapologetic about how we saw our calling together. Ultimately, God, the church, and even the community honored that.

Is it still a struggle ministering together, vocationally? Yes, of course. It is not easy to serve alongside one's spouse, at least it hasn't always been easy for us. Although at the moment we are employed separately from one another, there were times when church members have tended to see one or another of us as their minister. And this would cause conflict between us. Even so, we know we are both called and have been prepared well for ministry, as a unit working together or apart based what God has planned for us during a particular season in life. When one of us feels less important or significant, it hurts. It has been especially difficult for me, as I have sometimes felt that I was simply "riding Brian's coattails." Now, however, I am much more confident of my calling and giftedness, as is Brian. We are grateful for the meaningful ministry that God has allowed us to do through the years.

BRIAN & KIMBERLY MILLER reside in Greensboro, North Carolina, with Brian serving nearby as Minister to Families at Southeast Baptist Church in Greensboro and Kimberly serving as a Chaplain Resident at Wake Forest Baptist Health in Winston-Salem. They have three lovely children and have both been passionate about ministry since their teenage years. Each holds the MDiv from Campbell University Divinity School and a BA from the Baptist College of Florida, with Kimberly majoring in Christian Education and Brian in Theology. While both are pursuing ministry in their own areas, they continue to find ways to serve alongside one another. They are each other's biggest cheerleaders.

12

The Battleground of Tradition: "Holy Cow," Holy Communion

Jeffrey Steeber

"You have desecrated the most sacred celebration of Holy Communion! And that is why I am giving this council until the end of its meeting tonight to make this right. I will be calling Eric later, to see what you all have decided. If you do not reverse what Pastor Jeff has decided to do, then I will be submitting a petition to have you all removed from church council." As Mark made his way out of the meeting room, he slowly walked by me and said, "I'm sorry to have had to do this, but you brought this on yourself." And with that, the ten-minute presentation, rant, ultimatum-laced speech had ended.

In order to better understand how this claim was made against me, I will turn the clock back and provide some background. As I sat with the Bishop's assistant prior to accepting my first call right out of seminary, she laid out a few of the key issues that I would need to address. "First, this congregation was used to celebrating Holy Communion only once a month. Needless to say, it's 2006, and we don't follow those antiquated traditions anymore. So, the interim pastor got them to up Communion to twice a month, but we would like you to eventually try to get them to celebrate it every week." I responded, "Okay." "Second, they are still holding on to the practice of not giving kids their First Communion until they are confirmed. You should try to get them to understand that almost all of our congregations abandoned that way of doing things almost twenty years ago." "Okay," I said, "I think that I can take care of that too. I have this really good educational resource for our understanding of Holy Communion that I picked up during my internship. It helps people to see that the sacrament is a gift of God for all God's people . . . not just confirmed Christians."

About two months after I began serving my call, one of the parishioners, Walter, came to me with a question. "Are we going to keep having Communion twice a month, or are we going to go back to having it once a month?" "Well," I said, "We already have made the switch to having it twice a month, and from my understanding we have been doing that for over eight months, so we will keep it the way it is." "Sure," said Walter, "but when we made that change it was something that the interim pastor had put in place. To be honest, there were a lot of people here who just thought we would ride out that change until our real pastor got here, and then switch back." "Can I ask you a question, Walter?" I said. "Why do people want to go back to having Communion just once a month? In my home congregation, we celebrated it every week. Can you help me understand why you would want it only once each month?"

Walter thought for a second and then stated, "You see, when we had it just once a month, our attendance was always higher on the first Sunday, and our offerings were up too. So I think people liked that and want to get back to it." "Okay," I said, "so you want to switch back because the attendance and the offering were higher on the first Sunday of the month, which was also the one day a month that you could receive Communion?" "Yes," said Walter. "Well then, by that logic, we should be celebrating Communion every Sunday," I suggested, "because then our attendance and our offerings would be higher each and every week." Walter smiled back at me, finding my response humorous. "I get your point," he said. "Don't worry, Walter," I assured him. "I don't have any plans on making the switch from celebrating Communion twice a month to every Sunday . . . yet. I know that it will take some time before people would be comfortable with that big of a change."

For the two years that I served the congregation, we maintained our twice a month Holy Communion schedule. The original goal laid out by the Bishop's assistant was simply not realistic to me. However, I truly thought that I might be able to explain our Lutheran theological understanding of Holy Communion, and that the age for receiving it should not be linked with a youth's confirmation following the eighth grade.

I had been serving the congregation for about a year and a half before I decided to offer an adult education class on the topic of Holy Communion. It was not the first adult class I had taught at the church. I consider teaching to be one of my spiritual gifts, and I believe that Christians can never have too much education and information. I contacted the synod office with a quick email stating that I was going to be offering a five-week class during

Lent, in an effort to accomplish the second of the two stated goals that the synod office had for me before beginning my call. I posted fliers throughout the church building, wrote a newsletter article promoting the upcoming class, and made weekly announcements about it following the worship service. After the four weeks of promotion ended, I had 14 people signed up to take the class. At the time, our congregation was averaging approximately 115 people at our weekly worship. I was saddened but not surprised at the small number of people who signed up. I prayed that even though the number was less than desirable, those who attended (including several council members) would be receptive to the message and help communicate the material to their friends and family in the congregation.

The overall focus of the class was to discuss the origin of Holy Communion, how it has been understood in the church throughout the history of Christianity, and some of the basic theological concepts concerning it. The class met for five weeks, once a week for two hours at a time. In addition to the presented material, there was a good deal of discussion, questions, and personal stories. The individuals who were in attendance thanked me for teaching the class and for providing them with a deeper understanding of Holy Communion. I admit that I had an agenda in offering the class. The point was to help them see on their own, with some subtle (and not-so-subtle) suggestions, that our congregation should lower the First Communion age from eighth grade to fifth grade. Luckily, I did not even have to offer too many suggestions. Following the first few sessions, people started to openly discuss our current congregational practices. The "final straw" of the class was my simple, yet logically significant argument on the Lutheran sacraments, which I shall now provide.

Lutherans observe the practice of baptizing infants. Part of the reason for this practice is that we believe that the sacrament of Holy Baptism is solely a gift from God. The act is God's, and we are merely recipients of the amazing grace that God bestows. Our view regarding Holy Communion is similar in nature. The sacrament of Holy Communion is not dependent on or made valid by the pastor or by the person's individual faith. While we hold that a baptized individual is made "worthy" by believing that Christ's true presence in the meal is "For you," we also believe that we are simply recipients of God's grace and love. Therefore, my theological argument is this: We believe that God is the active Being in the sacrament of baptism, thus making it permissible to baptize infants because we are merely the benefactors of God's gift. Moreover, if we believe that God is the active

Being in the sacrament of Holy Communion (which is what we proclaim), then we likewise must find it permissible to commune baptized children.

At the concluding session of the course, many of those in attendance felt that we were called to offer the sacrament to all baptized children, instead of just lowering the communing age to fifth graders. However, the discussion eventually turned to a viewpoint that claimed that although the age for First Communion could be lower than the fifth grade, trying to make that great of an initial adjustment would not be prudent. At our next council meeting, I addressed the members and informed them that I would, with their blessing, lower the age of First Communion from the completion of Confirmation (eighth grade) to the fifth grade. I gave those who were not in the class a brief history of the sacrament, an explanation of our theology, and a summary of the discussion I had with the Bishop's assistant prior to my accepting the call. After I answered a few of their questions, the council agreed with the change in First Communion practice. I informed them that I would write a newsletter article that closely resembled the summary that I had just given them, and would make announcements in church about the change that would take effect in six months.

This brings us back to the night discussed at the beginning of this story. I met with Eric and Betsy, the council's president and vice president, respectively, in the hour leading up to the monthly meeting. At the conclusion of our executive meeting, Eric said, "Oh, I almost forgot to mention that Mark has asked to make a quick guest presentation at council tonight." I asked Eric, "Is he going to talk about the change in the age requirement for First Communion?" "Yes," Eric said. I knew that Mark's presentation would not go well for me or for the change in church policy. Mark, an older, lifelong member of the congregation, had not hidden his displeasure from me after news got out that I was making an alteration in Communion practice. He, along with several other congregational members, had taken to the community phone lines in an effort to spread the message that I was ruining the church. As the faction's leader, Mark was set on stopping the change from taking place. I had already received phone calls threatening a boycott on future financial offerings and church membership. I had done my best to respond to the threats by telling those speaking with me that I had offered a class, had received permission from church council, and, as the called pastor of the congregation, I was permitted to address and make changes to policies concerning Word and Sacrament (Lutheran pastors are ordained to the "Office of Word and Sacrament"). Nevertheless, Mark made his appearance at council, and he began his statement.

> Members of Council, I am here to offer my opinion, and the opinion of numerous members of our congregation, that Pastor Jeff cannot change our First Communion policy. According to our Congregational Constitution, those permitted to partake in the sacrament of Holy Communion must be "Confirmed Lutherans."

In this point, Mark was 100 percent correct. This was an issue that would be resolved by council, via a congregational meeting, over the next few months. He continued,

> I am amazed that you have all fallen victim to this man's decision to lead us astray from what we hold to be essential in our church. You have all ignored your duty to serve and represent the members of this congregation in an appropriate manner, and I cannot and will not stand idly by while you do so. Therefore, I am demanding that you overturn Pastor's decision to the lower the age of First Communion, tonight. If you do not do so, you are not only going against the wishes of various church members, but you are also going against our constitution. I am appalled at your lack of action in this matter, and you have caused many people to seriously doubt your commitment to leadership!

When Mark left the council room, the members, who had remained absolutely silent during the presentation, sat there with their mouths agape. "How dare he talk to us like that?" "That is not how you treat people!" "I cannot believe that he threatened to have us removed from council." "Well, you have to give Mark credit that he is not afraid to share his mind." And then they turned to me. "Pastor, what should we do?" I took a deep breath and smiled at them. "What can you do? If you do not overturn my decision, then we will be in for a huge congregational fight. Do any of you want that, for yourselves or for the congregation?" They all shook their heads and responded, "No." "Well then," I said, "I think you know what needs to happen tonight." Within the next two minutes, a council member made a motion to override my initiative to lower the age of First Communion, which was followed by a second to the motion, and ultimately a 10 to 2 vote in affirmation of the motion.

Note: The aforementioned story occurred as I served my first call. I am now in my third call, in Avon Lake, Ohio. I served my second call for four and a half years, and I did not leave under bad terms or experience any "out-of-the-norm" negative things while serving there. I remained with my first call for two years, and resigned/accepted my second call approximately one month following the events in the story. The names in the story have been changed, but the details have not.

JEFFREY STEEBER is ordained in the Evangelical Lutheran Church in America and serves as the Pastor of Christ Evangelical Lutheran Church in Avon Lake, Ohio. He holds the MDiv from Trinity Lutheran Seminary and a BA in Religious Studies from Kent State University. The proud husband of Melissa and father of Grace and Benjamin, he enjoys reading, watching movies and sports, and riding his bicycle.

13

The Cost of "The Call"

Courtney Pace Lyons

I remember when I first received my "call." I was fourteen, and as soon as my youth pastor said, "Someone in this room is called to ministry," my heart started racing. I couldn't explain it, but I knew he was talking about me. I had no idea *to what*, but I knew I was called. Long story short, I graduated from high school later that year and started college at age fifteen. I majored in Computer Science Engineering, but the most formative experience in college was my campus's Baptist Student Ministry. As I entered my senior year, everything I had planned for my future fell apart, and I had the terrifying opportunity of deciding what to do after graduation. I spent the summer as a short-term missionary in Vancouver, Canada, teaching ESL (English as a Second Language), and instead of getting a Master's degree in Computer Science, I decided to attend George W. Truett Theological Seminary at Baylor University to prepare for ministry. Going to seminary felt like becoming a Marine: "The Few, The Proud, *The Ordained*." We young ministers-in-training were excited that God had called us to do great things, and we were chomping at the bit to get started.

The day I moved to seminary, I was offered a children's minister position at a church near Waco, Texas. I had excellent role models for children's ministry from large suburban churches, but rural small-church ministry was very different from those experiences. I was accustomed to professionalism in worship, which is less important in rural churches. The pastor appeared supportive, but when a group of church members decided to run me off, he threw me under the bus. I resigned after eight months. Next, I served a medium-sized church as family pastor. This church purposefully targeted those on the margins: divorced people, recovered addicts, the tattooed and pierced, formerly incarcerated, and other "traditional church" misfits. I loved working in this welcoming environment, where societal divides fell apart and people worshiped as a community. I helped lead a Celebrate Recovery group and organized several family and marriage ministry events. I was heartbroken, though, when after I inquired about ordination, and was even approved by the elders to be ordained, the literalist hermeneutic of one church member halted the process.

A few months later, I became the youth pastor at an older, Caucasian congregation in a mixed-race community facing economic depression. The youth group was small, but as the kids brought their friends, we grew to several dozen every week. Our group was diverse in age, gender, race, and socioeconomic status. Adults in the church were partnering with the youth ministry, and I felt like we were doing real kingdom work. A small contingent—older white men—pressured the deacons to fire me, however, for "bringing in the wrong kind of youth." The attempt was unsuccessful, but I continued to face a lot of masked racism ranging from criticism of the youth's behavior, attire, and musical choices to complaints about the condition of the building after our meetings. By having the youth share testimonies in worship and participate in the choir, I hoped to build bridges between them and the adults in the church. Instead, the choir voted itself "Adults Only," and the new pastor actually kicked one of the youth out of the church.

I preached my first Sunday morning service on Mother's Day of 2007. I was grateful for the opportunity, but I realized that I preached on Mother's Day because there was fear of having a woman preach any other Sunday. I preached again the next year on Youth Sunday, again with mixed emotions. When I inquired about ordination, the ranking deacon asked me not to pose the question for fear it might split the church. After two years of ministry, a seminary degree, 1,000 percent growth in the youth group, hospital and nursing home visits, phone calls, late hours, and early mornings, they would not even entertain the question of my ordination. I love Baptist local church autonomy, but I hate how it can enable sexism.

When I was in need of a job after graduating from Truett, a seminary friend suggested that I apply to be a hospice chaplain. Hospice changed my life. There is rich beauty in helping someone die with spiritual peace. Many of our patients had not been able to attend church in years and longed to receive Communion or to sing their favorite hymns again. Some wanted to make amends with their relatives, while others wanted the ministry of prayer. Realizing the preciousness of spending time with someone who knows his or her days are numbered, I found freedom to speak intentionally about faith in a way I never had the courage to do before.

When I was accepted to Baylor's PhD program in Religion, I struggled with whether to stay at the church or resign. To do well in graduate school, I needed to be a full-time student. Leaving my youth was one of the hardest decisions I have had to make. They were my kids. For two years, I had picked them up in the church van, helped them with their homework, taken them on outings, watched their band concerts, helped them apply to college, and counseled their families. I hosted sleepovers, took the girls shopping before summer camp, and taught one of the girls how to drive. I actually intervened in a gang fight to protect one of my youth, twice. I knew that God had called me to teaching in Christian higher education and that I had to get my PhD in order to fulfill that calling, but my heart broke when I had to tell my youth that I was leaving. I still talk to most of them, and my heart lights up when they call to tell me how they're doing. I have also been humbled by God's faithfulness to provide loving adults in that church who have sustained and grown the youth ministry in new and wonderful ways.

In 2008, I began PhD studies, specializing in Church History. Believe it or not, but when I entered seminary, I leaned towards fundamentalism. But thankfully, Dr. Ruth Ann Foster opened my eyes to a richer kind of faith that sought understanding and worship over legalism and control, and my feminist awakening began. As I studied race and gender in American religious history, I found myself being further awakened to the pervasiveness of racism and sexism in the church, especially in conservative evangelical churches. Southern Baptists were some of the worst! As I better understood sexism and its subtle forms, I took the journey Dr. Rosemary Radford Ruether described in *Sexism and God-Talk: Toward a Feminist Theology*, where I realized how sexism and racism had affected me personally. I gave myself space to reflect on this, and then sought reconciliation with myself for putting up with it for so long. This process was incredibly alienating, and some relationships did not survive. Dr. Teresa Fry Brown calls this God's pruning process for those in our lives who won't support our call to ministry. Being a woman called to ministry is costly.

When I began my doctoral program, I was a lay minister in a small, rural congregation just outside Waco. There were two deacons, one from each of the controlling families in the church. The church previously had more deacons, but after a significant issue arose, all but these two deacons resigned. New families had joined who were excited about missions and discipleship. The power struggle between the old and the new families was crippling, however, and the handful of people willing to serve were worked to exhaustion but given no say. Most of the church opted for neutrality to avoid getting hurt (again), and I felt caught in the crossfire. As a minister, I wanted reconciliation, but I also realized that some people would never change. The leadership of this church was not open to new ideas, new people, intellectualism, or women in ministry, and I felt powerless to effect change or help the wounded.

Looking back, I did a few things right. I started a Sunday school class for the new families, where we sat in a circle and discussed the material together as equals. (The other classes were taught in lecture style by members of the controlling families.) My class responded well to our conversations, and I appreciated hearing their voices and watching them learn from and with each other. We built trust and respect, and we created an environment where we could discuss and even disagree without threatening our commitment to each other. As I made contact with the class throughout the week, I encouraged them to stay in touch with each other, and I delegated little responsibilities (attendance, snacks, prayer requests, etc.) to group members. I noticed that they started taking ownership for other things in the church, and I hope that what we did in our class gave them a foundation for speaking up and getting involved in ways that might have intimidated them before.

One example of this empowerment was a couple that joined the church a few months before I did. They started a small group in their home. One of the group members divorced her husband, and without asking her about it or offering to care for her, the church leadership stoned her—removing her from children's ministry, requiring her to attend Sunday school (taught by one of them), and refusing to give her a timeline for restoring her to leadership. This small group surrounded her with love and mercy, gave her a safe space to share her story, and went to bat for her. After more than a year of trying to reconcile, this woman chose to leave the church. I was delighted to attend her last Sunday to support her decision and to affirm that abuse in the name of Christianity, by a husband or a church, is never acceptable.

The power of this small group motivated me to try the same thing at my next church. It was a church plant located in a multiracial, poor neighborhood crippled by drugs, and with an extremely diverse membership. On any typical Wednesday night, there might be a recovering addict, an ex-con, a new Christian, a single mother, an immigrant, a retired minister, various blue-collar workers, and old church ladies. What a challenge to facilitate a Bible study discussion that could engage everyone! I loved it. I loved posing

questions that provoked meaningful conversation, and seeing the group
members teaching and learning from each other. I loved how they formed
relationships with each other outside church, erasing social divides that
might have prevented them from being friends. I loved how they cared for
one another and helped each other. I loved the vulnerability of our conversations, that they felt comfortable to share their deep questions and think
together about how to be the hands and feet of Christ in their community.
While at this church, I also had the opportunity to mentor the youth pastor
and offer pastoral support to several other staff. I was grateful that I could
give spiritual and practical encouragement to them as they were beginning
their ministries.

I know that God made me to be a teacher. Teaching Religion at Baylor
University, I have the privilege of helping students understand and consider
their faith with new eyes, to worship God with their hearts *and minds.* I
often find that students are afraid to ask questions, especially about God,
for various reasons. Some have been raised in legalistic faiths that accept
tradition without question. Some are afraid of the answers to their questions and so they dare never ask them. But the way I see it, any God worthy
of our devotion is big enough for all of our questions. Asking questions is
a way to understand God and Christian faith more deeply, to enter into
genuine faith that can accept uncertainty and mystery. I treasure these
precious, formative conversations, whether in class, discussion groups, or
mentoring relationships, in which I can affirm students' willingness to do
the hard work of articulating questions and seeking answers, and of inte-
grating *all* of who they are, both sacred and secular.

I love introducing students to the voices of the fathers *and mothers* of
the church, voices that have pondered questions of faith and the meaning
of Christian living. Students often think they are the first to ask their questions, and when I can point them to ancient voices that share their questions,
I feel like I am showing them a deeper community of faith along with the
faithfulness and consistency of God over time. As we discuss Augustine,
Teresa of Avila, John Wesley, or Martin Luther King, Jr., I emphasize the
issues that drove their writings so that students can understand that the
church has been formed and shaped throughout its history by people who
asked questions and sought deeper understanding of who God is and what
it means to be a Christian.

I have served in congregational ministry for over ten years, although
I have never been an *official* pastor. Even without the title, I have a flock

of people who see me as precisely that: *their* pastor. I have former hospice patient families who still call on me for pastoral care, and former students and parishioners who seek me for spiritual guidance. While I always encourage people to become involved in a local church and to transition to new pastoral staff, I am honored that they find our relationship meaningful and that I have an opportunity to serve them pastorally, whether for a season or a lifetime.

Part of my journey of faith and learning is social justice activism. I study civil rights and women's rights, and I have come to understand social justice activism as Christian orthopraxis. For me, this means speaking up against sexism, racism, and classism, and affirming women in ministry. Several seminaries are incredibly supportive of their female ministry students, but after seminary, even the best-intending schools can only do so much to help with placement. Clergywomen are making tremendous gains in networking with each other to streamline efforts and resources toward promoting women in ministry, and I am grateful to be part of Baptist Women in Ministry, The Young Clergywomen Project, and Equity for Women in the Church. I hope that those who support women in ministry will continue to do so *publicly*.

I have also become an activist for ministry motherhood, as my son was born during my PhD program, and, through a parental leave policy that I wrote the year before, Baylor allowed me to take maternity leave. However, some in my church had little patience for my new responsibilities as a mother. I either had to fulfill my pastoral role while carrying my son, or I had to arrange for childcare. I got dirty looks for nursing on site, and even dirtier looks for bottle-feeding. Thankfully, for others, sharing the experience of parenthood forged new connections and deepened our relationship. I am deeply committed to supporting fellow mothers in ministry and am grateful for the growing number of ministry moms who are refusing to separate family and work, but instead are modeling a new way of being their real, whole selves.

It happens that seminary did not turn out to be like the Marines, but as I entered congregational ministry, I realized that ministry really sometimes can be like going to war. Churches sometimes beat you up so bad you are not sure if you can get back up. People you thought you could trust, even some you know from seminary, can betray you so deeply you don't know if you'll ever heal. Church leaders do terrible things and get away with them, while tragedy repeatedly strikes the dearest of saints, and when someone asks you why, you may find that you have no answer to give them. I have cried heaving sobs from the depth of my soul, not even sure what to pray, but knowing that God's hand was the only thing left to grasp.

No minister, young or old, can survive alone. So in realizing that, I am a proponent of being authentic with your congregation and letting them see who you really are, but I wish I had realized the importance of having a spiritual community *outside* of your congregation earlier on. I am blessed by two best friends, fellow women in ministry, who are my spiritual community. We are completely open and honest with each other about everything, and I could not survive without having the safe space that we share. We have supported each other through betrayal, divorce, lost ministries, new ministries, and everything in between. Whatever comes, we are there for each other. They are my spiritual guides, my confidantes, and my *sheroes.*

Another life lesson I wish I had embraced earlier in my ministry is the importance of self-care. I train as a figure skater, but I used to feel so guilty about "wasting" half a day that I could have used serving my church. Now I realize the importance of having a creative, physical outlet, of having an identity wider than ministry, and of doing things that I enjoy. Skating renews and recharges me. I have more energy when I get off the ice than I had when I got on. There will always be visits to make and more research to do, but we need to take care of ourselves, spend meaningful (not left-over) time with our families, and do things that make us feel joy. If we don't take care of ourselves, we will run dry quickly. And this neglect of self helps no one.

Reader, whether you are new to ministry or a seasoned sibling of the cloth, my prayers are with you. May your joys and accomplishments be turned to praise of the One who called you. May your heart be wise enough to protect you from harm, yet vulnerable enough to allow love and hope to abide richly. May you delight in activities and relationships that renew you and remind you that the world is a wonderful place, and may you be immersed enough in reality that you remember that you are but a speck of dust preaching *foolishness.* May your spirituality be like a blossoming tree, rooted in God and bearing much fruit. May you be obedient to that which God has called you, no matter the wilderness in which you find yourself. And may you never lose hope that God restores what is broken, finds what was lost, and is always faithful.

COURTNEY PACE LYONS is Assistant Professor of Church History at Memphis Theological Seminary in Memphis, Tennessee. She holds the PhD in Church History from Baylor University, the MDiv from George W. Truett Theological Seminary at Baylor University, and a BS in Computer Science Engineering from the University of Texas at Arlington.

Clergy > 35

14

The Racial Context of Christian Churches in the United States

David F. Evans

"The details and symbols of your life have been deliberately constructed to make you believe what white people say about you." —James Baldwin

One month before my spouse and I arrived at our first pastoral appointment, the chair of the church's Pastor, Parish, Relations Committee informed our congregation that they were receiving an interracial couple. When I asked why she singled out that particular detail to share with the congregation, she replied, "Because I want people to be aware of potential issues." I was quite certain that she would not have shared the racial composition of two white pastors. It angered me that she felt that my marriage was a "potential issue." After I reconciled with my indignation, I allowed her preemptive signal to the congregation to remind me that race in American Christian churches is not a neutral issue. This provided me the capacity to accept a basic truth: race matters in US Christianity, and my ministry will need to address that truth.

In this essay, I identify overt racially charged church spaces in Christian history as reminders that Christian communities ascribe value to racial categories and reinforce those racial values in symbols and rituals. Social conformity to racial assumptions, local and denominational, is not mere window dressing; rather the stained-glass windows of churches often reflect the expectations of the dominant society in which they exist. I am reminded of this fact each time I see Warner Sallman's 1924 depiction of Jesus' white face that decorates the walls of many Christian homes and churches. Indeed, many Christian communities are so comfortable with racial categories that they do not question the Western racial assumption that all of the prominent people in the biblical narratives looked like Europeans.

The racism that exists in churches is deeper than outward appearances. Racism is only cosmetically a problem of prejudice against people with darker skin pigmentations. In its most significant manifestations, racism is the systemic and institutional power to favor one racial group over others on the basis of perceived physical features. This particular component of racism is sometimes difficult for Christians to comprehend. A Christian friend confessed to me her guilt for considering the possibility that her Christian place of employment showed signs of systemic evil. She felt that Christian institutions were too deeply Christian, or good, to be guilty of such an accusation. She wanted to believe that evil in a Christian institution could not be systemic, only cosmetic. She was not naïve about difficulties that arise in Christian contexts. Certainly, she knew of rogue pastors who stole headlines for ungodly reasons. She knew of church leaders involved in scandals, doctrinal debates, and church splits. However, the idea that the church could be fundamentally flawed threatened her faith, and she felt guilty for entertaining the thought of it. Her ecclesiology defined the church as pure and blameless. Hers was a pristine view of the church that believed a perfect and blameless structure lay underneath the veneer of human sin.

Churches are not perfect and blameless. My experience, both as a pastor and as a seminary professor, tells me that Christian institutions are produced by the societies in which they dwell. As a historian, I assume that churches are not solely divine institutions; they are also social ones. Though divinely inspired, churches are human made and human filled. They are co-constituted by social realities: legal, political, national, gendered, and racial. As such, churches are shaped by those systems as much as they shape them. Often, it is the case that churches become the last bastions of social stagnation, as was the case with many white moderate churches during the Civil Rights Era when their clearest message to freedom fighters was "wait." It is a rare Christian institution that leads society against social injustices. One reason for this is that many congregations have sought, at one time or another, to be accepted by the societies in which they dwell, meaning that their doctrines and polities reflected the dominant philosophies and categories of their social context.

The social context of the United States has been shaped largely by the racial conflict initiated by white society's claims of superiority and resistance to that notion by people of color. Perpetuating the dominance of white Protestantism, however, is not solely the work of white Christian institutions. The most recent depiction of white Jesus that I witnessed in a church setting was in my hometown African Methodist Episcopal congregation. As a United Methodist, fully aware that I help comprise the 4 percent African American membership of my white-dominated denomination, I was surprised when I opened the front door to the AME church to see that the first face to greet me was not black; rather, I saw the face of white Jesus framed on the wall. This AME church is not alone in its allegiance to the blond-haired Jesus of Western Christianity. One can also witness the relationship between a black denomination and white Jesus at Mother Bethel AME in Philadelphia, Pennsylvania, when rays of the sun shine through white-skinned and blue-eyed Jesus in windows that depict the Savior. My point here is that the literal window dressing of white and black denominations in America often affirms the warning James Baldwin gave his nephew in *The Fire Next Time*: "The details and symbols of your life have been deliberately constructed to make you believe what white people say about you."[32] In the context of a racially constructed society, darkness and light take on epidermal significance, so the idea that even the words of Scripture, "in God there is no darkness at all," sends a clear racial message; God is white.[33]

Segregated Symbols

The music of American Christianity does not provide much resistance to this claim. Hymns like the theme of Billy Graham's famous crusades, "Just as I Am," and the classic, "Nothing but the Blood," make darkness a proxy for sin and whiteness the goal for every Christian life. With the reality that song is more memorable than sermon, the messages of these hymns have tremendous effects for shaping Christian ideas.

It is not always necessary to make the symbols of Christianity explicit in their racial connotations. When twentieth-century evangelist Billy Graham first initiated his crusades, the architecture and theology of the gatherings made racial interpretations commonplace. From 1950 to 1952, Graham led crusades in southern cities where the organizers assured Graham that the audiences were segregated. When pressed to explain why he did not protest racial segregation in these situations, Graham responded, "We follow existing social customs in whatever part of the country in which we minister."[34] As was the case with many white evangelical leaders, moderation was key with Graham at the time. For those years, racial segregation provided the context for the second verse of "Just As I Am."

> Just as I am, and waiting not
> To rid my soul of one dark blot,
> To Thee whose blood can cleanse each spot,
> O Lamb of God, I come, I come.

There is certainly nothing explicitly racial about this hymn, but the repeated refrain defines darkness as dirty and sinful in the racial context of white over black. Moreover, in the context of segregated seating and segregated society where darkness is a feature ascribed to the bodies of black people, it is not difficult to hear the song as an implicit endorsement of the segregated situation, wherein darkness and light had no fellowship.

Though Jim Crow laws are no more, racial segregation in Christian communities continues. What do darkness and light metaphors communicate in racially segregated audiences? This is not merely a question for the past. A 2007 Pew research study found that only 7 percent of US congregations are integrated. In addition, as of 2004 US schools were as racially segregated as they were at the time of the 1954 *Brown v. Board of Education* decision that struck down Jim Crow laws and the legal opinion "separate but equal." This means that US Christians are living in de facto contexts that connote racial inequality, and the music of Christian congregations too often reinforces that notion.[35]

Christian symbols and songs that reinforced racial inequality fueled Nation of Islam leader Malcolm X to name Christianity "the white man's religion." In 1963, Malcolm explained in his "Black Man's History" speech, "My father was a black man and my mother was a black woman, but yet the songs that they sang in their church were designed to fill their hearts with the desire to be white."[36] His most frequently used song example was the hymn "Nothing but the Blood," which he mistakenly referred to as "Wash Me White as Snow." His confusion was understandable considering the hymn's chorus, which includes the phrase he found most problematic: "Oh! precious is the flow / That makes me white as snow . . . ."

Malcolm recognized that many Christians despised his comments, so he challenged them to do some reflecting. "Rather than get resentful," he recommended, "all they have to do is think back on many of the songs and much of the teachings and the doctrines that they were taught while they were going to church and they'll have to agree that it was all designed to make us look down on black and up at white." One could certainly object that the language of the hymn reflects clear biblical imagery from the book of Isaiah. However, in the racially charged context of Jim Crow, Isaiah's first chapter call "to seek justice" was rendered racially mute, while "though your sins are like scarlet, they shall be white as snow" seemingly justified racial arrangements.[37]

Race and Ritual

Racial arrangements, while visible and audible, in the architecture and artistry of images and hymns were only outward expressions of deeply held beliefs and practices. In the nineteenth century, the social reformer Frederick Douglass declared that racism was so deeply ingrained in US Christian church life that he could not call those churches Christian. "Between the Christianity of this land, and the Christianity of Christ," Douglass wrote, "I recognize the widest possible difference—so wide, that to receive the one as good, pure, and holy, is of necessity to reject the other as bad, corrupt, and wicked." He clarified his criticism by referring specifically to the US Christian practice of holding slaves and defending slavery. Still, his autobiography, *Narrative of the Life of Frederick Douglass*, demonstrates that slaveholding provided only the basis for color prejudice in churches and hardly the totality of it.[38]

In 1841 Douglass began a speech, "The Church and Prejudice," to the Plymouth Anti-slavery Society with two damning stories of Eucharistic practices to show how deeply institutional racism had penetrated his denomination. Holy Communion is arguably the most significant liturgical witness to unity between believers. For Douglass, however, it was a symbol of disunity and racial injustice. Through his first story, he shared a personal account at a church that ultimately led him to forsake Communion at that particular congregation. He described watching as the minister served all the white members bread and wine. Next, after taking a deep breath, the minister called the people of color forward, saying, "God is no respecter of persons!" Douglass was appalled by the contradiction between the actions and words of the congregation and never returned to that church.

Douglass narrated the second story as an observer. A young woman of African descent was present in a white church during Communion. Due to the presence of a white abolitionist, the minister could not move the cup past her lips and gave her the shared Communion chalice. When the pastor presented the cup to a white woman who sat next to her, the abolitionist's presence meant nothing; the white woman rose up and walked away, refusing to drink from the cup. Douglass chastised the hypocrisy that he witnessed by emphasizing that the white woman who sat next to her was "baptized in the same water, and put her trust in the same savior, yet when the cup containing the precious blood which had been shed for all, came to her, she rose in disdain, and walked out of the church. Such was the religion she had experienced!"[39]

One hundred years later, James Baldwin questioned the same sacramental waters of US Christianity in his novel *Go Tell It on the Mountain*. In a powerful climactic moment, Baldwin describes his protagonist's vision of a black Pentecostal Communion scene full of women and men dressed in long white robes breaking bread and drinking wine, but their feet were bare and bloodied. Following in the Last Supper tradition, they tried to wash one another's feet in a basin, "but the blood would not wash off." Then they struggled over one another to get to the river for baptism: "The strong struck down the weak, the ragged spat on the naked, the naked cursed the blind, the blind crawled over the lame." Neither the basin nor the river could clean their bloodstained, ragged, tattered robes, leading the reader to wonder, "Does this water wash?" Is the Christian religion, with its rituals and beliefs, powerful enough to root out the fear and violence of racism in its churches? Though he put forth the question via fiction, one can certainly read Baldwin as making a theological and practical point about the power of racism in US Christian congregations.[40]

Conclusion

Future ministers and current church members cannot afford to pretend that the religion of US Christianity is pure and undefiled from systemic evil or that racism only exists in some white supremacist congregations. Those who do will continue to be surprised when they face institutional symbols and structures that perpetuate racism in the churches. They should not be surprised, however, because as church architecture, art, classic hymns, activists, and authors have demonstrated, the foundations of US Christianity were constructed with the same tools and materials that made the US a white supremacist nation. The reality that today Jim Crow segregation is illegal—racial discrimination is punishable by law, and the US currently has an African American president—changes the context of this history, but not its legacy. That is, white people developed US Christianity for white people, making some amendments along the way. While one cannot ignore substantial challenges to white Christianity by daring innovators throughout history, Christianity in the United States reflects the Western trajectory of European theology and practices with all of its racial trappings. To ignore this is to pretend that somehow Christian doctrine and practices are too set apart to be affected by social contexts and are above social accommodation.

My spouse and I were blessed to find that social accommodations could change for the better; no one in our first church objected to their co-pastors on account of their interracial marriage. However, had we sought welcome at First Baptist Church in Crystal Springs, Mississippi, in 2012, it is likely we would have received the same rejection that an African American couple did when they attempted to wed there. This couple received news that the church would not marry them, though they had already sent out invitations and up to that point heard no indication that there was a problem. According to *ABC World News*, the church had never married a black couple in its 119-year history. The congregation made certain that Te'Andrea and Charles Wilson's wedding would not be the first. While the rejection sounds like a centuries-old tale, the threat of job loss and fear of conflict that led to it are symbolic of endemic racial ideologies in American Christian communities of the twenty-first century. While the white pastor, Stan Weatherford, was willing to marry the couple at the church, where Te'Andrea Wilson's uncle was a staff member and her father was a member of the congregation, the white members of the church threatened to fire Weatherford if he did so. Instead, the pastor married the couple at a nearby black church to save his job.[41]

American Christian churches, black or white, are racial institutions that operate in and through racial contexts. Whether intentional or not, the symbols and structures of US Christianity are racially charged symbols and structures with all of the consequences such arrangements produce. The first step in dealing with the devastating impact of racism—that mutes the liberating message of the gospel and renders churches ineffective to deal with deep racial divisions—is to recognize how substantively concepts of race have penetrated Christian behaviors and beliefs. After this recognition, Christians can begin to reconstruct their institutions in a way that might truly wash away the stains of racism.

DAVID F. EVANS is an Assistant Professor of History and Mission at Eastern Mennonite Seminary in Harrisonburg, Virginia. He holds the PhD in Historical Studies and Master of Philosophy from the Graduate Division of Religion at Drew University, Master of

Theological Studies from Wesley Theological Seminary, and a BA in Christian Ministries from Spring Arbor College. He is an ordained Elder in the United Methodist Church.

15

A Love/Hate Relationship: My Bipolar Experience with the Body of Christ

Jay C. Hogewood

If the opposite of love is not hate but indifference, as some wise soul mentioned to me years ago, then I employ the word "hate" shamelessly. If this greater work is indeed about telling the truth, then both—love *and* hate—are completely truthful to describe my regard for the church as well as church folk. I say both without apology.

I love the church.

I hate the church.

I trust you might know what I mean.

I confess that there was rarely a time while growing up a Baptist in Birmingham, Alabama, that I wanted to go to church. I had accepted the lordship of Jesus at fourteen, and on most days I actually tried to deepen my devotion to Christ. Rarely did that effort have anything to do with attending church. I did go along with my parents before they split up, and then I went with my dad through my teenage years. But "youth group" was thoroughly intimidating, and, though I loved Jesus and was as moralistic and self-righteous as a teenager could be, church was the Virgin Bride: beautiful and pure, even eager to be adorned by my backside in a pew, but she was never giving, always aloof.

When I entered full-time ministry, I was twenty-seven, full of energy and wide-eyed wonder. I had experienced the "call" as a young married man at a wonderful Methodist church. My first love for church may have been akin to "puppy love." Still, that kind of love gave God enough room to work. From initial crush to full-fledged relationship, when I look back, I see that it all happened so fast. Those first few years through seminary and doctoral studies, along with serving churches, I simply had no background as a participant in a congregation when I rather suddenly held leadership within one.

A handful of moves to various Baptist churches (Texas, Ohio, and Louisiana) stitched together with a few more years of theological education meant I was growing in the role of minister. I encountered functional churches and dysfunctional churches (funny how they always share the same address). I admit that I participated as much in the dysfunction as the function. So over fifteen years of ministry as an associate minister at larger churches, then as the pastor of a medium-sized congregation, my relationship with churches and church folk was in full swing. I have noticed a few hallmarks in this relationship. While I am hardly an expert in the field of *ecclesiology* that I was taught in seminary, I can reflect on what I have encountered in congregational life. But you need to know this much about my life: I write these thoughts as a broken minister, bearing fractures I can no longer hide—fractures I no longer want to hide.

Destructive Tension

By age forty, I crashed and burned, resigning from the pastorate, so tired of congregants who declared, "We want you to lead us" and "Help us grow bigger." While I would offer my best leadership, my most faithful preaching, my deepest levels of energy, and what felt like the guidance of the Holy Spirit in response, the very same people would push back, saying things like, "Well, we don't want to try that" or "We want to keep this the same." Insanity distilled: we keep doing the *same* things expecting *different* results. If insanity had a face, it was definitely church. Doing church work, I felt like I was going insane too. I was drowning, my life crashing like waves, one on top of the other. Ministry, I have come to believe, offers this dangerous invitation to life in one dimension, where I felt like I was swimming in the fish bowl for all the world to see with no one else willing to jump in and swim with me. Instead, everyone else felt welcome (even entitled) to come by, tap on my glass home, maybe even drop a bit of food for me to gobble up. Watch that little fish swim. And swim I did. For my life.

All the while, as waves of career and calling and ministry tossed me in the growing sea of resentment, my life as a husband felt increasingly isolated. The intimacy I desired with my spouse, I tried to extract from the congregation. Transference gone bad, let's say. The patterns of our communication and our sexual intimacy were so dehydrated, so malformed, so deadened by years of neglect. We were highly functioning as cohabitating parents. She was successfully earning a second Master's degree. I was enjoying effective marks of growth in the denomination and in the community. On the face of things, our world looked fine. But deeper at the core of our lives, I knew better. We encircled each other but were so rarely present for each other; we seemed for so long to be perfecting the art of "just missing each other."

She felt distant from me.[42] I felt distant from her. Unhealthy. Unbalanced. Unsatisfying. Unmerciful. Unrelenting. Undone. I was ready to float away. So I did. Floated away by resigning from ministry—a "calling" for which I had invested over nine years of my life in academic degrees and mentored relationships that amounted to God knows what. Floated away by separating from my wife. We ultimately divorced after eighteen years of marriage, and then I played a new role, a role I despise about myself—the chaos-maker who ruptured the home that my two children used to know and enjoy.

If we are really telling the truth here, I blame the church as a major source for my brokenness. At the same time, I also credit the church as a massive support for my healing, for helping make me whole again. I have, after all, what might be termed a *bipolar relationship* with the body of Christ. Ups and downs. Push and pull. Attraction and repulsion. Euphoria and depression. I have experienced tensions that are creative and those that are destructive. I love the church. I hate the church. Here are two primary reasons.

Authenticity/Inauthenticity

Church is ideally the place I want to "get real," and church is composed of the people with whom I want to "be real." Who better to be real with than those of us who come to grips with the reality that we are simultaneously sinners and saints?[43] The problem, however, is that sometimes when I was most vulnerable, I found that it only took one person in a group to use my vulnerability to hurt me. Then we continue to create the *myth of fine*. "I'm fine," we say when someone asks, "How are you doing?" "They're fine," we respond when someone asks, "How are your kids doing with your work schedule and school events?" "We're fine," we lie to those who ask seriously or casually, "How is your family in the transition to the new church?" The *myth of fine* is the path to inauthenticity.[44]

I remember leading a Bible study on Proverbs. The couple dozen older adults who participated were overwhelmingly supportive of me, especially as I shared my own challenges as a young father struggling to find the time to help coach my son's soccer team. Unfortunately, one of my ardent critics weeks later recalled back to me that my use of time was not what it ought to be if I was to be a good pastor. Specifically, she used my own struggle with time to pierce my pastoral role. "You should consider spending more time doing your work than worrying about coaching," she said in cold blood. So much for authenticity, I thought. Why share my life if what's shared is only going to be blasted back at me?

The tension in this part of the relationship has to do with choosing when and where to be authentic or vulnerable. Because I'm a slow learner, it took me far too long to realize that by sharing aspects of my parenting in a prayer meeting or in conversations with church leadership, I was opening ways for a few coldhearted congregants to offer criticism. I am reminded that even though these instances might be the vast minority of our experiences as ministers, it only takes a few harsh words from just enough people to jeopardize our desire to be real, to share struggles and joys. The challenge to being authentic is the desire instead to be fake, to be inauthentic. Most of us would admit that we live with fakeness in our world as people who prefer falsehood to truth.[45] I confess that I participated in the effort to be authentic until it cost me, until I got burned. I regret that my fragile ego cut me off from a longer effort toward authenticity. After a few instances of having my authentic self diminished, I tucked my tail and ran back to inauthenticity. Being less than authentic may offer me less reward, but I figured it demanded less risk anyway.

The poles that make up this part of the potential bipolar disorder of a church can create a positive tension. I mean, if the majority of folks know and trust that we gather to be real with each other about our sin, our struggles, our fallings and failures, then church invites us to transparency and to *real* community. Sadly, I find that it only takes one person to turn positive tension into destructive tension. And unless other congregants are willing to confront the person bent on destructive criticism, I noticed how much energy and time I lost confronting this person on my own. Then peace is sacrificed in community, as it was in my own life.

"Peace is built on truth."[46] Truth, which requires the risk of being vulnerable, builds up the community of faith. When I felt threatened for sharing the truth of my life with certain fellow Christ followers, it pains me to confess that being fake became a much easier reality in which to minister, where the *myth of fine* prevailed over being honest with congregants about struggles and celebrations in life and as a fellow disciple of Jesus.

Connection/Disconnection

An older, wiser minister friend once said that we are all like electrical cords with our prongs sticking out, ready to be plugged in. We all want to plug in with others we admire. Our prongs (being known, being accepted, being loved) are eager to connect—to be charged and replenished. The beauty of this possibility in the life of a church is the *reciprocity*—the give and take—of such relationships built on truth: as we seek to know others, accept others, and love others, we also receive their gifts of allowing ourselves to be known, accepted, and loved.[47] Unfortunately, as I felt my grudge grow against a few people in the congregation, I let my own sense of violation morph into disconnection. When my charge was depleted, I began to seek other ways to replenish.

The poles of connection and disconnection are a particular challenge to me. On one hand, I believe the community of my church is called by Christ to be the place for the greatest, deepest connection. Isn't that at least part of the gift of the church empowered by the Holy Spirit (see Acts 2:42-47)? This is the creative tension of community in Christ—we share a unique connection to those with whom we worship Christ and serve in his love and power. But once I felt that being fake was safer than being authentic, I realized I wanted to pull the plug of my own connection. Then, on the other hand, the tension caused by disconnection meant I wanted to connect with others who would really know me, accept me, and love me.

There are healthy ways we go about this—connecting, as ministers, outside the relationships we have with congregants. Clergy friendships across denominational lines can be vital in this regard. Relationships cultivated in sports teams, community events, and other common interests also hold great potential for healthy connection. Other loving relationships are certainly invaluable for mutual connection—marriage, committed and intimate friendships, and partnerships come to my mind. The thing is, I didn't seek them. Honestly, I simply didn't expend enough energy to make those better, healthier connections.

I confess that I made mistakes in this way. I connected with others who abused my trust and whose trust, in turn, I violated. Because I felt my own marriage was unhealthy, the disconnection from my spouse was a painful reality I chose. In the tension of connection/disconnection, I highlighted my own destruction. Instead of allowing the tension to help me be more creative with godly connections, I tucked my head down. I didn't cry out for help either loudly enough or consistently enough. I felt like congregational life piled enough sand in my ocean of resentment for me to have my own island. I swam out to it, pitched my tent there, and died to ministry. Not as a martyr—not even close. I died to ministry as a failure.

Creative Tension

My story in ministry could well have ended there. Death *in* ministry. Death *to* ministry. The poles of authenticity/inauthenticity and connection/disconnection pulled too far and tore me to pieces. The tensions within congregational life were more destructive than constructive. And I was the central player making more bad decisions than good as my experience ministering to a congregation unraveled.

I am grateful to share that in many ways, my story actually does not have a happy ending; yet that is only because I write not from the ending but from a new beginning. Through Christ's gracious work in a congregation and a remarkable friend in the United Methodist tradition, I have a second chance. My own pastor, Dr. Van Stinson, was an instrument of God's reconciling love. He refused to let me pull away, to sit on that island of my own sin and despair. God used church folk to restore my calling and to bind together my brokenness. I confess that I am a work in progress, of course. By the mercy of Christ, a church acknowledged my fractures of sin but did not stop there. That congregation and its minister reminded me of the very promises I used to preach: that sin has consequences, yes; and that God grants second chances a thousand times over. The work of Jesus Christ to forgive sins and restore relationships applies to everyone, even me.

This relationship with church shattered me.

This relationship with church pieced me back together.

I am grateful to say that many things have changed in my life over the last four years of this renewal of "call." After the resignation, the death of my marriage, and the grief and shame of admitting failures to my children, I was not sure where to turn. I had lost my footing. For a couple of years, I worked as an insurance agent. And over time, with the love of my son and daughter supporting me, I returned to a congregation. It only took a few months before I became deeply involved in that vibrant community. They encouraged my gifts and reinforced my calling. I also rejoice in a second chance to marry again. In the parking lot of that very church at our youth ministry's carwash, I met a wonderful woman whom I love dearly.

Over the last year, I have entered ministry as a vocation for the second time, and the United Methodist Church (UMC) has extended amazing grace to me as I now pastor a growing congregation in my hometown.

While I wish like mad that the tensions within congregational life were always creative and positive, I have enough sense to know otherwise. Still, God works among us and through us. Jesus calls. The Holy Spirit moves. And this time around, I pray that I learn from mistakes and love the church as the hurting/healing body of Christ.

JAY C. HOGEWOOD is the Pastor of Ingleside United Methodist Church in Baton Rouge, Louisiana. He holds the PhD in Hebrew Bible from Brite Divinity School at Texas Christian University, the MDiv from George W. Truett Theological Seminary at Baylor University, and a BA in English and History from Samford University.

16

Surprises and Challenges in the Blessed Office

Kirsi I. Stjerna

Twenty-something

I was twenty-six years old when I was ordained. Looking at the pictures from those days, I understand why the word "girl" was used in reference to me, even when I hoped to look so grown in full clerical uniform. I have sympathy for that young, innocent girl in the pictures and her uneasiness with the many things inherited when stepping into the pastor's (historically male) boots. For me there had not been any role models for female pastors, or young pastors for that matter. I had only known male pastors with gray hair, so I thought of pastors as father figures. Even now after all these years, I still sometimes wrestle with boots that don't quite fit, wondering about this whole identity issue, which is to say how was/am I supposed to be a minister? I am still facing some of the same struggles that took me by surprise as a newly ordained young woman: the constant need to be on guard against attempts to be patronized, controlled, dismissed, or simply seduced. I also still face the challenge of feeling my limitations and small-ness in the face of the enormous task called ministry. Being young and female and among the first wave of ordained women in my home denom-ination added extra weight and unforeseen challenges to my first years as a pastor. In retrospect, my youth and naïveté probably protected me to a degree and provided the crazy courage to take on the challenge. In retro-spect, it is probably not a coincidence that I took a break from ordained ministry after just one year. The predominant memory of that first year is of being, to put it lightly, slightly unprepared.

My home church, the Evangelical Lutheran Church of Finland, began ordaining women in 1988, quite unexpectedly after decades of debates.

Some of the women had been praying for that day and in tears accepted the symbols and powers of ordained ministry. So many were under thirty, fresh out of university with minimal experience in the daily demands of the pastoral vocation. Most of us had actually not even thought about ordained ministry that seriously, as it had not been a real option, and then suddenly, *boom*, the door was opened and we were called to serve! None of us knew how to "deal" with things that would come with ordained ministry, or how to be a "lady pastor," as we were affectionately called.

There were times when people would explicitly request the "new lady pastor" or, just the contrary, would demand a "real" pastor, that is, a male pastor. Quite a few times people came to church or to an event to check out the female pastor. Sometimes attendees apologized for having doubted that "a young girl like you could do such a fine job." And then there were the ill-advised, unfortunate men who found themselves morbidly attracted to the young female preacher. The latter, of all the challenges I encountered, was perhaps the hardest one to bear and the most surprising. I had assumed that that the pastoral office and ecclesial gear with its heavy, silver cross created a protective neutral shield and de-sexualized things. But I was wrong! People who had been in ministry before us knew better, thus the outfit created for the female pastors came with stern orders for how to *dress down*. No butterflies in the pantyhose, no high heels, and only small earrings and modest makeup, please.

It was decided that women should not wear the same outfit as men. Why? I don't know. Perhaps that early overnight decision reflects the lingering ambiguity over the issue of women in ministry to begin with and resonates with the centuries-old headache over femininity and female sexuality that has had unfortunate, negative connotations in the world of theology and male clergy's imaginations. A top designer was hired to create a clerical suit for women. Made of heavy, dark wool material, it consisted of a knee-length skirt and a white "pastoral blouse" to be worn with a rectangular jacket that covered breasts, possibly pregnant bellies, and hips, and did its best to hide any femininity, thus creating an illusion of age or agelessness. The suit was made with an older female character in mind, one without a style or sexuality. Yet, though well intentioned to protect the women in ministry, the suit quite certainly added to the identity confusion of the younger women who were not prepared to give up their youth and gender for the sake of effective ministry, as the mandate to wear the outfit may have implied. In my memory, the suit encompasses many of the issues I faced as a young female pastor, the biggest of them being perhaps the confusion of my identity: Who am I as a female pastor? Who am I supposed to be? Can I be that? How can I be me, a woman, and a pastor? And do I need to grow old(er) overnight to have any credibility? Ironically, the lady pastor's suit became my best friend for the time being; while it effectively hid my personality, and to a degree suppressed my gender/sex, it also added to my years.

Can one be effective as a pastor when one is young and inexperienced in life? I wonder about that when I send off my students each year. I teach at a Lutheran seminary where we train pastors and teachers, and after many years of teaching mostly second-career students, I find that a stream of younger, twenty-something candidates is entering the ministerial track in larger numbers. I watch my students filled with fire eagerly embrace their calls, feeling invincible like Joan of Arc, willing to go nearly everywhere. They love to preach, are committed to serve their fellow human beings and perform the sacraments, and hoist upon their young shoulders the many responsibilities the pastoral office demands. They smile at some of the issues we "older" folks warn them about, such as sexism, racism, and elitism in church; they typically start their careers with a somewhat naïve constitution of things being so much better for their generation, which leaves them often utterly unprepared for the stings of -isms they will, unfortunately, encounter sooner or later. When hitting the class ceiling in employment policies for jobs with the highest pay and authority, or when facing the lack of support for maternal leave and family time, a disillusioned woman will appreciate what the feminist "fuss" about women's rights has been about.

Also, whether male or female, in their burning desire to serve in the office of a pastor, the newly ordained pastors often neglect to look after themselves from the get-go and to do all they can to protect the well-being of their families. Regrettably, the church is not always the fairest employer but may take advantage of people's earnest sense of vocation and Christian virtues of humility and poverty. A young pastor asking for a higher salary or vacation package and retirement benefits is easily frowned upon and doubted for his/her spiritual fortitude. Knowing this and eager to get a job, a younger pastor is not likely to stand firm in the negotiation stages to secure a fair salary that would keep one from sinking into debt or to win reasonable arrangements for parenthood-related needs.

This leads me to a most painful subject—how hard it is to serve the church and thrive as a parent. This is an area where younger pastors have a calling and an opportunity to make some changes, to benefit themselves and those to come. Young pastors can break the spell and end the tradition that still, in many places, rests on the model of celibate male clergy, and they can reshape ministry vocations so that models for healthy family relations and parenthood, when applicable, are an essential part of the picture. Also important, young pastors have the challenge of modeling how to be a pastor and single without the medieval yoke of celibacy set on them. I'm talking about Protestant churches that do not consider marriage a sacrament and that, generally speaking, celebrate clergy marriage and do not condone celibacy, and yet tend to expect celibacy from their unmarried clergy, young or old. For young pastors who are not married or wish not be married, this is a tender issue that definitely affects their quality of life. The situation is especially complex for pastors who are gay and whose church does not "authorize" living out their sexuality or bless the committed relationship beyond heterosexual marriage.

Thirty-something

I returned to parish ministry in my thirties after jolly times in graduate studies. This time I was married with a child. Both aspects clearly added to my credibility as a person, and the baby served as a brilliant icebreaker for those not yet sure about female pastors. Innocent grinning infants prove to be a powerful argument for women pastors! At the same time, it was quite a learning curve for the congregation to have not only a female and young-ish pastor but also a nursing pastor. The same is true for me too: I was walking in uncharted waters, and graced by the acceptance and support of many wonderful individuals who were growing with me and expanding the horizons of what ministries and ministers can entail.

On the home front, I was blessed to have support with my child and served only part-time, while I was fully aware how difficult things would have been had I been hired full-time. The competition between church life and family life is unfair, and the former tends to win. This is true, especially in situations where the good-old male pastor model still applies, with the spouse expected to maintain the home hearth and care for the children while he attends to the congregation's unending needs—very much after the model of Martin Luther and his wife Katharina von Bora. Today that model hardly works for either male or female pastors. If we practice what we preach, we need to be actively present in our children's lives. That would seem like a no-brainer, and yet in many situations serving the church is not always conducive to a satisfying family life. Just think of the number of regular and unexpected evening meetings and, of course, weekends and major holidays devoted to church service. It is not bad—just a reality to reckon with. I remember, fondly, my toddler learning to walk in a Worship Committee meeting. Saturdays we all carved out for weddings, funerals, and baptisms. The sermon and worship preparation involved the entire week and gave a particular rhythm to Saturday nights. Christmases were special; I remember nursing between services, with no time to cook or wrap gifts, feeling like a guest in my own house at Christmas, and worn out, but not in a bad way. There was beauty in all that though fulfilling the pastoral role required sacrifices.

My solution to the everyday challenges as a mother and a pastor was to bring my infant with me whenever possible to the office, to home visits (vigilantly protecting her from picking up pills from homebound patients' floors), to hospital visits, to ceremonies (when allowed)—you name it. Day after day I rocked the baby's crib while typing sermons, rushed into work during her precious and generous naptimes, and burned candles from both ends trying to get up before anyone else and stay up way after everyone else's bedtime, so that I would have time for my child during her awake hours. Even working part-time, I felt the pressure and can only imagine had I been the full-time pastor: the pitiable arrangements for maternity leave or childcare or in general for working conditions of young parents in my church would have made it extremely difficult to mother my child the way I saw best in my situation. Of all the issues that burden pastors, younger ones in particular, this is the most pressing one.

After parish ministry, I moved to another kind of ministry with a more administrative nature. My call required traveling and long days at the office, which I resented, as did my children. Much of the work I could have done from home with my computer, but the office policy was such that staff members were present in the office, Monday through Friday, from morning until late afternoon. I remember having my computer space blasted with images of my children, and rushing in and out in the daily commute to maximize family time. I think I cried every day out of guilt. I missed my kids. Yet I loved what I was doing and had a sense of needing to be in that place right then. Sure enough, from that call I moved on to full-time teaching. My call as a minister in my church today is that of a teacher. I consider myself lucky as a family person: teaching ministry has enough structure and enough flexibility to better attend to my family life than I was able when in parish ministry or in the administrative position. This is of course my experience and not true for all. Yet I believe the problems with parish ministry and family life are well known due to the nature of the call interwoven with life's surprises in general.

The personal price is too high not to worry about this issue for future's sake. The fact is, we never get back the time we lose, and with our children, we don't want to be on the losing end. Not only do the children suffer, but we as pastors suffer too, as we may become bitter towards the very people we wish to serve or become alienated from our own families. If I could go back in time, and if I was to seek a full-time job in ministry, I pray that I would have the support, courage, and fortitude to negotiate working conditions favorable for families with children. Having said that, as a mother of two children who are now teenagers, I can also happily attest that the minister's life does allow a certain level of flexibility that persons working 9-to-6 jobs do not have. With priorities in place and support from the congregation—sans emergencies—one can exercise more control of the schedule that allows her/him to be regularly involved in children's lives in many delightful ways.

Forty-something

I thought I had experienced it all in the church until I entered yet another stage: divorce. Unfortunately, what is true in society in general is also true in church: women who divorce are often treated with utmost suspicion. The church's conflicted teaching on divorce and sexuality crystallizes in a situation when a female pastor is suddenly single. What unresolved issues and tensions congregations have around issues of sexuality, gender, and divorce may unfairly flare up when a younger, once-married female pastor is suddenly man-less. This experience has made me appreciate the plight of female pastors who are single and under scrutiny on account of their lifestyles more so than their male peers. Married with children is still the unspoken norm in many places. If a woman is not married or, whether married or not, if she has no children, or if she is divorced, she may bear taunting, unsolicited questions, comments, and speculations, all of which have a direct impact on her happiness and the effectiveness in her call to ministry. In areas of the quality of human life—single or married, with children or without children—the church could lead the way towards healthier attitudes and ways to support people in different situations with different lifestyles. With young pastoral leaders who are confident, healthy, and visionary in this regard, there is hope.

In Retrospect

I fear that I have written with a tone of complaint. I considered it my task, however, to illustrate from my own experience areas of trouble in ministry for younger persons, as a fair warning for the young entering the noble calling, with the best of intent. As a teacher of future pastors, I see men and women, young and older, prepare for and enter their callings. I see a great variety of spiritual and personal maturities, as well as different kinds of treatments pastoral candidates experience. My heart goes out to the female candidates who often are subject to questions and directives that middle-aged male candidates would never need to bear. Questions about weight, number of pets, sexuality, marriage plans, appearance, and general capabilities are not uncommon with female candidates. Younger females are also often placed in more supervised positions, as if needing more protection and guidance, even if these candidates are among the very best and most qualified. From my perspective, the ageism is not quite as big a concern as the frustrating lingering sexism. For that, all ministry candidates, young and older ones, should properly prepare themselves.

Thinking of myself as a twenty-six-year-old entering ministry, a while back, I know now that I was unprepared for some of the tasks and prepared for others. Yet in my youth I had energies and resources and unashamed confidence that allowed me to enjoy the rollercoaster and ride on the waves. What helped me personally was my Lutheran theology: the conviction that my ministry's blessing or my effectiveness as a pastor is not ultimately about me but about God, and that I am a servant, equally sinful and holy in Christ with the people I serve, young and old. That theology and centering on God's work carried me through, rendering my age and gender irrelevant in the larger picture. That theology allowed me to contribute in important ways, even when I was so finite, not so skilled, and not always prepared for what was to come. What also supported me in my journey where the amazing people I got to know—children, teenagers, adults, and the elderly. I count it a privilege to walk by and with people through different life situations. In these relations, I learned to take on slightly different personal roles while being carried by the ageless office of a pastor.

I am convinced that the future of Christian churches is in the capable hands of the new young servants to come. In God's crazy plans, the church does not need to be perfect, the pastors do not need to be of "right" age or sex or orientation or maturity, but God uses all of us as is fit in God's design. I thank God for the brave, spirited, curious young people who experience the nudge that calls them to try ministry and who are bringing with them new vision, new challenges, and new paths to take. For those readers, I hope, the issues lifted up here are not a deal-killer but rather pose a welcome challenge to tackle.

KIRSI I. STJERNA is the First Lutheran, Los Angeles/Southwest California Synod Professor at Pacific Lutheran Theological Seminary of California Lutheran University in Berkeley, California. With ordination credentials from Evangelical Lutheran Church of America and the Evangelical Lutheran Church of Finland, she holds the PhD in Theological Studies from Boston University, Master of Theological Studies from the University of Helsinki, and BA from Lyseon Lukio College. Among other books, she is the author of *Martin Luther, the Bible, and the Jewish People*, co-edited with Brooks Schramm (Fortress, 2012); *No Greater Jewel: Thinking of Baptism with Luther* (Fortress, 2009); and *Women and the Reformation* (Wiley-Blackwell, 2009).

17

Living & Leading with a Grateful Heart

Jane Williams

I write this during the most satisfying time of my thirty-plus years in ministry. My current work draws from my experience and training as an Episcopal priest and licensed psychologist, and gives me opportunity for creativity as I develop ways of forming and guiding my students. I mentor and supervise counseling interns, work with ministry interns in their provision of pastoral care, and introduce students to the practice of ancient spiritual disciplines. Had you asked me at my ordination what I would be doing in the final ten years of my ministry, I would never have guessed it would be this, and yet I believe God guided me in unique directions that have allowed me to integrate and use my experience and training in behavioral science and theology in a healing ministry that has typically remained outside the walls of a church.

I first heard God's call to ministry when I was a teen. I grew up United Methodist at a time when the UMC was far more liturgical and Anglican than it is presently. My father and grandfather were both ordained in the UMC—my grandfather as a lifelong local church pastor and my father as a pastor and later a chaplain in the Veterans Administration. Being female when I knew no female clergy, I thought God was calling me to teaching or nursing in a missionary setting as a deaconess. When I arrived at college, however, professors encouraged me to pursue secular vocation, and so the call to church vocation faded away. At the same time, I discovered a new denominational home in the Episcopal Church. It felt like a homecoming. The mystical experience of liturgy; the emphasis on Eucharist; the use of the body in kneeling, bowing, crossing oneself, using incense; the Via Media tradition that allowed me to explore and question but not be judged—these fed me in ways the UMC's drift into evangelical praise services did not. The Episcopal Church's choice not to ordain women at the time (1968) was not an issue for me. I was content to discern a secular vocation and participate in worship as a lay reader and acolyte. When eleven female "renegade priests" were ordained in Philadelphia in 1974 (canonical approval for women's ordination was finally granted by the General Convention in 1976), I did not pay much attention.

Having graduated from college Phi Beta Kappa with a liberal arts degree in 1971, the initial years following were a time of discerning a career path in social service, considering graduate education, and settling into married life. Only two years into the marriage, however, my husband died suddenly. I was nine months pregnant. Left with few financial resources and emotionally unprepared for single parenthood, I moved in with my parents and, after my daughter's birth, went back to work in local government social services.

The shock of being widowed left me spiritually devastated at first, then opened me to a need for a more personal experience of God's love and presence. I craved and needed worship, but even more I craved and needed God's love incarnated in human flesh. And God supplied. I was invited into a relational small group-oriented organization called *Faith at Work* and became part of the Women's Team that planned retreat weekends for women. There I found a family of five "sisters" who were committed to a lay ministry of creating opportunities for women to find faith and hope through relationships with each other. Our "Women's Circle" eventually let go of retreat ministry but has continued to meet in our sharing circle for thirty-five years!

God's love was incarnated as well through relationships in my childhood UMC congregation where my parents still attended. Several older women of that congregation reached out to me, throwing a baby shower, mentoring me as a new parent, encouraging me with stories of their own struggles through loss and single parenthood. Most moving of all, however, was their complete and total acceptance of me and of my daughter, Jess. I felt deep shame about my husband's death because it resulted from an overdose of illegally obtained drugs. Rich was a pharmacist and, unknown to me, became addicted to narcotics. He was about to be fired from the pharmacy when he committed suicide. I kept these circumstances secret from everyone until, with deep shame, I confessed the truth to these women. To my surprise and great joy, they did not change demeanor or behavior when I shared the truth with them, but only wrapped me tighter in their love and

God's love. It was an experience of God's grace incarnated—an unexpected gift.

Still, as a widow at age twenty-eight, I felt very alone. I didn't "fit" in widows' support groups where the average age was late fifties or early sixties. I didn't "fit" in young adult groups at church, either; they were couples-oriented, and I felt like my experiences and challenges weren't in sync with theirs. And the secular Parents without Partners seemed to be far more focused on finding a new partner than on helping me cope with single parenting. Then, in a magazine I happened to pick up, I read of a woman my age (twenty-eight) whose husband and two-year-old daughter were killed in an accident when she was a few months pregnant with a second daughter. She had just published a diary of her experiences through her grief and the first years of her daughter's life and of how her faith was challenged and changed into more than simple belief. Paula D'Arcy's book was a lifeline for me. Her experience of grief mirrored mine so closely that when I met her thirty-three years later, I felt like we were sisters. Her faith, like mine, had been challenged, had survived her anger and doubts, and had become stronger and more honest as the wounds of loss began to heal. What was tragic and devastating, God used for good.

My daughter's birth was a gift to me in the midst of grief. And living with my parents was a gift for them as well, as they found deep delight in my daughter. Previous differences in lifestyle, politics, and values became less important than guiding and loving this new life together that had been given to us. My teenage brothers and my mother and father delighted in Jess, and she was surrounded with love and play. Through such grace-filled synchronicities, I began to see God's presence in my life in a new way. And in my gratitude, my heart opened once again to the whispers of a call. I could no longer dismiss such things as coincidences, but saw them as confirmation—*signs*—that God was calling me to use my life with all its ups and downs to help others. God had comforted me through Scripture and relationships, and now I was hearing God's call to comfort others with the comfort I had received. God was helping me to see a purpose—a precious way to make meaning—even out of the pain of loss. I had no idea how God would use it, but I was sure God would.

When Jess was eighteen months old, God stirred my heart to love again. Ken was a UMC minister who loved us both—a "package deal," he called us. His ministry was focal for him, and he saw in me the helpmate and companion he had wanted for so long. I loved him, and I also saw the possibility of living out my call through his ministry in the United

Methodist denomination. (I had still not allowed the thought of ordained ministry into my consciousness and felt that God was calling me to serve in more traditional roles for women: Sunday school teacher, counselor, all-around "whatever you need" pastor's wife.)

We had only just begun to settle into our marriage and parish when, just weeks after our one-year anniversary, Ken showed me several swollen glands on his neck. He had no symptoms of a cold, flu, or sore throat, and both of us thought it was some minor infection. A checkup the next day at the family clinic in our small town assured us that the swelling would go away with prescription antibiotics. Three weeks later as we lay in bed, I felt a small lump on his chest . . . then another and another.

"How long have these been here?" I asked.

"I just noticed them this morning. I was hoping they'd be nothing, but you can feel them, too?" Ken answered.

Neither of us slept well that night. Ken went back to the doctor's office first thing in the morning, and the look on his face when he returned told me this was something to worry about.

The clinic doctor immediately placed a call to a local internist. We were told to go to the internist's office, even though office hours were ending. We didn't know at the time that "last appointments" of the day are usually given if the patient is likely to receive difficult news. No other patients would be in the waiting room to see tears or witness crying. As the three of us (Ken, three-year-old Jess, and me) drove there, Ken and I tried to "read" what had upset the clinic doctor. Our first thought was cancer. But how could it be? We were probably just worried over nothing, we both reassured each other, hoping our inner fears weren't too apparent to the other. I was thinking that surely God wouldn't allow cancer to disrupt a new marriage, a new parish assignment, and the life of my young daughter who had already had enough loss in her three years.

Office staff took blood and vital signs, and showed us to an examining room. Ken sat silently on the examination table. I sat on a chair beside him with Jess on my lap. Jess was cranky and wanted my attention, but all I could do was hold her tight. I know she sensed my fear.

I wondered if we had been forgotten as the minutes ticked by, and then the specialist entered with his chart of test results. He examined Ken's chest, groin, armpits, and then spoke softly and slowly.

"I am so very sorry. You have non-Hodgkin's lymphoma, cancer of the lymph nodes . . . an advanced stage . . . very serious . . . likely terminal . . . a month . . . chemotherapy . . . hospitalization."

I wrote down as much of what he said as I could. He gave us time for questions, of which I had many. At the end of thirty minutes that seemed like a year, we were given the name of an oncology/hematology hospital practice in a city an hour away and urged to get Ken into the hospital that evening.

As we drove home to collect PJs and an overnight bag, I held Jess close. I was too angry for tears—angry at God. I had considered myself "safe" in some way. Surely being widowed and pregnant at twenty-eight was the worst that could ever happen. Yet, here Jess and I were again, facing imminent loss (perhaps no more than a month away) of my beloved.

We were told it was not possible for stage 4 lymphoma to remit, but Ken surprised everyone. After the first course of chemotherapy, he went into remission for a glorious and intense twelve months. For the next four years, we lived with intermittent relapses (lymphoma is now highly treatable, but at the time it was almost invariably fatal at stage 4).

I struggled with clinical depression, and entered therapy to cope. What my therapist, a wise Jewish woman, said to me during a session when I was particularly stuck on "why God is doing this to me again" began to guide my reactions to Ken's illness and impending death in a different direction.

"You will ask 'why' over and over again until you no longer need to—that's normal," she told me. "One day your question will begin to change, and you will begin to ask, 'What can I do with this to make it meaningful?'"

Her simple wisdom laid the foundation for my ministry ever since. What could possibly make the loss of two husbands by the time I was thirty-five meaningful? What could make sense of the suffering Jess endured with these losses and the struggles she continues to go through as an adult trying to trust that significant others will not abandon her? What could make meaning of my diagnosis of breast cancer at age forty-five? Or my mother's thirteen-year descent into Alzheimer's disease early in my father's retirement? Or my sister's severe mental illness that required institutionalization in her teens and resulted in her death at a young age? My ministry has been a journey to learn how I might use the comfort and healing that God gave me to help others struggling with their own deep suffering.

In the months after Ken's diagnosis, God's whispers became words I heard not only in my heart but also from the mouths of three parishioners within a week: "You should be a minister. Have you ever considered it?" I entered Drew Theological School (UMC) eighteen months after Ken was diagnosed. I managed full-time study in the first two years, but by the third year, it was obvious that Ken was succumbing to the relentless onslaught of lymphoma. I dropped classes and picked up some of Ken's preaching and worship responsibilities at church. Helping shoulder a few pastoral duties allowed Ken to continue his appointment to the parish, which meant we could keep living in the parsonage and be covered by his medical insurance and salary.

Most parishioners understood that. However, parish systems can react to stress and loss in bizarre fashion depending on the parish and individuals' histories. As Ken weakened that fall and I became more visible, a few church leaders began to gossip that I was acting inappropriately for a grieving wife—that I should be home with Ken and Jess (and that he should retire) and that I was obviously not taking care of him. My motives were questioned and I was rumored to be having an affair. In an already painful time of loss, God helped me overcome my conflict-averse style and ask for a chance to talk face to face with those who were slandering me in the presence of church leaders. The main rumor spreader admitted that her accusations were lies, and asked my forgiveness. I learned how powerful truth could be when combined with forgiveness, and the parish leadership wisely chose to involve a consultant to assist the congregation in its grief.

Ken died on Ash Wednesday, a cold, snowy, early March day. The symbolism of dust and ashes resonates deeply with me each year.

Most parishioners shared our grief and looked for ways to support Jess and me as a way of honoring Ken. The church hierarchy (in the UMC), however, was most unsupportive. My District Superintendent (DS) visited a few days after Ken's funeral and told me that I should begin packing for Jess's and my move to a new parish—that she would be appointing me to a student parish in two months. I was stunned and numb. I had just lost my husband and Jess had lost her father! My therapist supported me in not making changes to our lives during the next year. I knew we would need to move from the parsonage, but I naïvely thought we could remain in the only community Jess and I knew—the community that had supported us these past four years. I did not have the energy to work while grieving, finishing my Master of Divinity, and being a mom to a hurting six-year-old. Angrily, the DS told me that women pastors have to do things that would not be expected of male pastors—that we have to be strong for our sisters in ministry and show that we are not weak. If I turned down a student appointment this year, she said, she would give me the last possible parish appointment when I graduated. I declined the student appointment. I knew I had nothing left to give. And the DS was true to her (vindictive) word; I received the last parish appointment the following year.

In the ensuing twenty-some years, my call to ministry and my search for "what will bring meaning" to the experiences of a lifetime have led me "back home" to the Episcopal Church and to ministry as an Episcopal priest in a variety of settings: in a college counseling center, in a pre-K through grade 12 school as chaplain/psychologist, in an urban parish as an assistant priest and coordinator/workshop leader in the parish-based spirituality center, in a thriving private practice as a licensed psychologist/pastoral counselor, and now in a seminary pastoral counseling program as director and associate professor. I have worked with young children suffering the loss of a parent, with teens struggling with sexual orientation, with college students coming to grips for the first time with childhood sexual abuse, with single parents and divorcing parents, with individuals and families facing chronic and terminal illnesses, with persons whose relationships are causing unbearable pain and conflict, with clergy disillusioned with what they thought was a God-guided institution.

I have been blessed to journey with people to the dark places of their lives. I can journey with them because I have experienced those dark places—and know that God dwells there, too. I hold the hope for them when they cannot see hope for themselves, just as countless others held hope for me when I could not imagine surviving what was happening in my life. This is what my ministry is, as I understand it.

Ministry has been most difficult when dealing with the dysfunctional politics of the institution of the church, and so I discerned early in ministry that my call was not to parish ministry nor to Diocesan administration, but to work I would do directly with folks who were suffering (churched and unchurched) to be a bridge leading to the One who helps us find hope and meaning in whatever life brings. Ministry has been most rich in counseling those who struggle and suffer and are in deep pain for whatever reason; such struggles and pain no longer hold fear for me, and I am blessed that those who need to go deeply into their struggle allow me to accompany them.

It is not me who helps or heals them. It is the One who walked with and healed me who accompanies each of us on our own healing journey and who gifts us with strength to continue the journey until Light dawns again.

Some might ask why ordination has been important for me. Why not just leave the church and function as a layperson of faith? I would answer that despite the failings and shortcomings of the institutional church, and despite the pain it can inflict on its ministers, the church is guardian of

sacred vehicles of grace in the Sacraments. To be able to offer the sacrament of Eucharist, or of confession and reconciliation, is to be a channel
of God's grace and healing, and that is the most compelling reason for my
continuing in ordained ministry. I am grateful for God's call to service. I
am grateful for the fullness of life with which God has gifted me. And I am
grateful for those who honor me with their trust.

JANE WILLIAMS is an Episcopal priest and Associate Professor
of Clinical Counseling and Director of the MA in Clinical Coun-
seling program at Moravian Theological Seminary in Bethlehem,
Pennsylvania. She holds the PhD in Counseling Psychology from
Lehigh University, the MDiv from Drew University's Theological
School, and a BA in Political Science and Philosophy from West
Virginia University. An avid gardener, she loves to plant and tend
perennials, vegetables, and raspberries.

18

A Candid Confession: An Anabaptist Woman's Experiences in Vocational Ministry

Heather Ann Ackley Clements

I am a woman ordained to ministry of word and sacrament first in the Mennonite Church USA and now in the Church of the Brethren, both part of the historic Anabaptist tradition of peace churches derived from the "Radical Reformation." However, I also have much ministry experience, particularly in interfaith and interdenominational, ecumenical settings. Raised by "hippie" parents in the 1970s, one of whom was an atheist and the other agnostic, I actively sought spiritual wisdom in many religious traditions throughout my teenage years and was baptized just before my eighteenth birthday in a Presbyterian church uniquely consistent with my "hippie" values during the Reagan era—active in feeding without question anyone who was hungry, committed to peace, disarmament, and reconciliation, and welcoming to gay, lesbian, and transgender Christians. Within months, I was ordained for the first time, becoming a deacon of the church in 1984.

As a new Christian, I used my liberal arts education at a small Methodist college as an opportunity to learn about the Bible and historical Christian teaching and practice, especially to understand why my new wider Christian "family" of faith was experiencing so much conflict over sexual issues. I could not understand why *all* Christian churches did not practice peace, as well as welcome and offer practical care to society's poorest members as my own congregation did. By the time I graduated with my BA, I had accidentally minored in Religion, and my college chaplain and vocational counselors encouraged me to attend seminary. As a woman in the late 1980s and with my newly educated insight into the lack of faithfulness of so many US Christians in that time to Jesus' teachings on being peacemakers and the centrality of care for those who are poor, I dismissed this idea. At twenty-two, I had never met a female clergyperson. And this was after numerous years of exploring different faiths, denominations, and churches throughout North America and Western Europe, where I had studied for a year as a French major. However, my college chaplain's wife was the executive director of a parachurch organization founding a homeless shelter where families could live together (the first in our state) when I was about to graduate, and I volunteered to work full-time onsite in exchange for room and board. Within months, she stepped down and offered me her position, which the board of trustees affirmed due to their positive assessment of my contributions to their shelter.

As a young woman in leadership of a Midwestern parachurch ministry in the mid-1980s, I encountered much hostility and resistance from the other, much older woman heading the other major parachurch ministry in this college town, who publicly and privately chided my inexperience and perceived me to be in competition with her, though I meant to work collaboratively. Because Reaganomics hit this rural-industrial community of working-class people particularly hard, my executive parachurch job was only half-time, and I had to take on another half-time position at a second parachurch ministry, this time working as the executive director of a drop-in center for adults with mental illness. The chair of that board of trustees was a professional woman herself and was very encouraging and supportive, so this second position was a much more positive experience where I never felt that my contributions were tainted by others' negative perceptions of my age or gender. However, the first position was rife with so much conflict that, somehow blaming my own failings, I finally felt the call my college chaplain had earlier identified. I was now ready at twenty-three to pursue seminary education to be equipped for more effective parachurch leadership.

During my theological education at an interdenominational seminary in southern California in the late 1980s, I explored biblical scholarship (still looking for answers as to the confusing division in the church over sexual issues), church history, and the relationship between Christianity and other world religions and philosophies, and was introduced to theology. To fund my education and living expenses, I took on a supervised pastoral internship as the youth pastor of a congregation in a very liberal denomination with which I had no previous affiliation. Unlike myself, my supervising pastor and the congregation overall were quite wealthy. Though

I had grown up and worked only in multiracial, working-class communities up to this time, this congregation was predominantly white. I found the racial and economic homogeneity disorienting and jarring, not realizing at that time how typical this is in American churches. I was introduced to Women's Studies during my seminary education and (having been raised by a feminist activist mother and taking gender equality as a given) was shocked to learn for the first time that women had been excluded from church leadership, biblical reading, and theological education (both from learning and from teaching) for most of Christian history the world over.

This pain was deepened when my married, middle-aged pastoral supervisor, whose daughter was about my age, graphically described his physical arousal and sexual feelings for me privately in his office, which absolutely terrified me. I could not afford, however, to leave this, my only job at the time. Therefore, I refused his advances both in person and in writing, but stayed on. From the time I said "No" to him sexually, he acted very angry with me, verbally insulting me every time we met. He ceased all efforts to support my ministry with our youth and my ministerial education. So I abandoned my plan to earn a ministry degree (which would have taken an additional year) and settled for a Master of Arts in Religion, which afforded me to leave the job as soon as possible. During my last week on the job, I contacted the denomination about his behavior, and a female district supervisor encouraged me to file a formal report, mentioning that he had exhibited a past pattern of such conduct. This experience was so alienating and painful that I left Christianity altogether to practice Buddhist meditation and study the *Dharma*. However, with what seemed to be a useless Master's degree, I felt forced to continue graduate education in order to *at least* become a university professor. Though I hoped to study world religions, my previous formation in Christian ministry/theology and continued desire to study biblical teaching and confess my faith in Jesus Christ led secular graduate programs to reject my application. This was despite my summa cum laude academic marks. I was eventually accepted, however, with full scholarship and living stipend into a globally prestigious PhD program in philosophy of religion and theology, in which the faculty at that time were focused on Christianity.

During my doctoral education in the early and mid-1990s at this secular institution in southern California, because of my age and gender, I was frequently mistaken as a church secretary or institutional staff member by faculty and visiting scholars. This happened not only at the university and its libraries but also at professional conferences in philosophy and theology. In many PhD classes I was one of only two women students, and throughout the 1990s at most professional conferences with Christian emphases, I was either the only woman or one of only a tiny handful attending in a professional, academic capacity. When I graduated with my PhD in Christian theology, I was encouraged by the Anabaptist congregation with whom I then worshiped to become the senior pastor. Our current pastor left the state to pursue further ministerial education due to her lack of opportunities as a woman pastor in this denomination. In spite of my PhD and seminary degree, I was required to take additional denominational workshops and classes to meet specific licensing and ordination requirements, not only in the first denomination in which I was ordained in 1998 but again in a second, closely related Anabaptist denomination when I transferred my church membership and ordination status in 2011.

When the male chair of our church board of elders told me of the congregation's desire to call me to pastoral preaching and sacramental ministry, I was certain a mistake had been made. By this time, I had experienced so much gender discrimination and sexual harassment in the church and theological education that I felt I was fit for nothing but teaching in a secular university where I might hope feminism had made some inroads. However, my husband at the time encouraged me to discuss the opportunity with our conference minister (the equivalent of a bishop)—a male—so I did. All parties dismissed my anxiety about my gender. Almost angrily, the conference minister asked me who I was to stand in the way of the Spirit calling and equipping whomever God wills to ministry. So shamed, I reluctantly became the pastor of this small house church of pastors, bishops, and seminary educators. My ministry there was always affirmed, encouraged, and supported by all but the husband of the former pastor, who (I think rightly) did not feel I was qualified for this leadership position because of my age (thirty-one) and inexperience. I spent one year as a licensed pastor and, after completing all additional ordination requirements and meeting with a supportive but all-male search committee, was ordained at thirty-two. However, the demands of my dual vocation to pastoral ministry and university teaching aggravated marital discord as my successes (becoming published and speaking at national professional conferences) far outstripped those of my high school-educated, working-class husband. As he became increasingly hostile and verbally abusive in front of our young daughter and I increasingly spent time away from home, our marriage ended in divorce. When I announced our separation to the congregation, they terminated my employment, creating not only deep emotional anguish but also tremendous financial strain as I was solely responsible for our daughter's support and care as a newly single working mother.

In my mid-forties, my ministry was largely channeled into faith-based teaching of Christian theology and church history at a Christian university. I began my full-time teaching there after adjunctively teaching Hebrew, biblical hermeneutics, and church history at a predominantly African-American, charismatic Bible college in a Christian community where women's leadership and teaching were common so that only my youth, inexperience, and minority race were occasional issues. Thankfully, I never experienced gender discrimination there. However, once employed for teaching pastoral ministry and introductory theology at the predominantly white, nondenominational, evangelical university (where most students and faculty were at least upper middle class), I was constantly questioned by both fellow faculty and students about how I could possibly consider myself qualified to teach ministry as a woman. My pastoral experience was most often summarily dismissed as irrelevant by both students and colleagues. Despite my educational and professional qualifications, including publication, I was hired at the lowest possible level normally reserved for adjuncts, a step or two below the less-qualified male colleague hired in my department at the same time. Each year, I had to reapply for my job as the only female candidate for the position and sometimes as the only full-time female faculty member. I had the enthusiastic support of the department chair, but I frequently overheard insults of my teaching and presence from students, staff members, and faculty. To them, my solid teaching evaluations (from both students and supervisors), service to the university, and continued success in national presentations and publishing didn't matter much. This hostility didn't diminish until I asked to move from teaching pastoral ministry to church history and systematic theology full-time. In my university teaching, I am able to give significant attention to discussing issues of discrimination on the basis of gender, race, economic class, culture, and ability/disability with students and colleagues, both in classes and as the long-time chair of the faculty senate's diversity council.

Even so, issues of theological exclusion continue to affect my ministry during my middle age, as many colleagues and denominations read the Bible and Christian history differently than I do on issues of human sexuality. I have found diverse opinions on this matter to be considered by many Christians insufficiently faithful to Christian orthodoxy. Though less often than at one time, I still receive hate messages via voicemail and e-mail from Christians offering statements about how they are offended by my ministry and teaching as a woman, because they believe women are forbidden to speak publicly to any adult male about spiritual matters. Being considered an apostate by those for, with, and to whom I minister has contributed to my adult struggles with clinical depression, which I have sometimes self-medicated with alcohol and sometimes medicated with drugs prescribed to treat my low mood and suicidal ideation. During my employment at the university, after my termination in pastoral ministry, I was hospitalized for almost two weeks in a psychiatric facility for treatment for addiction and depression, and I continue to work a spiritual program of addiction recovery with the help of female Christian mentors. My program and those who participate in it are mostly Christians who also have been wounded by fellow believers, through rejection and verbal abuse, and thus are now angry with Christianity as a whole.

Today I remain committed to sharing the gospel of the radical love and grace of God expressed by Jesus Christ as best I understand it. Though I feel called to do this within the Christian community in the church, as well as through writing and teaching, I recognize the real possibility that I may one day be forced out of the church and the Christian university by theological exclusion and discrimination.

HEATHER ANN ACKLEY CLEMENTS is the former name of H. Adam Ackley, a transgender professor of relingous studies at the University of Redlands in Redlands, California, who began to identify as male after submitting this essay. A third-generation northern Appalachian migrant, Ackley is the author of *Women, Music, and Faith in Central Appalachia: Studies in Women and Religion* (Edwin Mellen, 2001) and co-author of *Daughters of the Mountain South* (University of West Virginia, 2009). He holds the PhD in the Philosophy of Religion and Theology from the Claremont Graduate University, MA in Religion from the School of Theology at Claremont, and BA in English and French from Mount Union College. Ordained first in the Mennonite Church USA, Adam is now an ordained minister in the Church of the Brethren and works as an educational consultant and freelance writer.

19

The Spiraling Journey of Baptism, Confirmation, and Ordination

Christopher D. Rodkey

Introduction

The summer of 2009 was a turbulent time for me; its imprint is still fresh on my soul. The economic downturn led my wife to be laid off from her business that relied heavily on the credit industry. We had just moved, I had accepted a new call, and we had bought a house a few months earlier. We had also decided this would be a good time to have another child. My mother was hospitalized with some heart problems and my elderly grandmother was simultaneously hospitalized off and on. They were actually in the same hospital at the same time. When I went to visit, I made a wrong turn and found myself stopped by security, as I had accidentally wandered onto the pediatric ward, which years ago was their maternity ward. As I quickly left the area, I realized it: *I was born here.* After a reflective pause, I visited my mother and grandmother.

During the drive home, suddenly my wife didn't feel well. She knew something was wrong with the baby. We turned the car around and headed back to the women's hospital in Lancaster, Pennsylvania, and after hours of waiting, we learned the devastating news: our prenatal baby had died. We didn't talk about what had happened. We cried, held each other, and argued, but we never really talked. Internally, though, I had experienced in one day a transfiguration—while staring at the possibility and inevitability of the loss of family members, we simultaneously lost the latent potential that lived in my wife's belly, and I myself gained an introspective spark of my own origins. I have often contemplated the reality of my own death, but I had never seriously thought about the experience of my own birth.

This experience of loss also taught me how fortunate I am to be loved by my family and close friends. I had always thought of love as something that just happens, something you do. Because I love you, for example, I do this or that which I would not necessarily do for someone I don't love in the same way. Or, because of my fidelity to God—or *in spite of my fidelity to God*—I extend an act of love to you as a stranger, but my relationship might end with this single act of love. We are making love or we're not making love. Love is an action, not a metaphysical or purely theoretical condition.

My congregation was enormously supportive during this time of loss. We had not long before revealed her pregnancy to them, when my wife could no longer hide it especially from our nearly three-year-old son, who could not restrain himself from pointing to her tummy, proclaiming, "There's the baby! *In there!*" My parishioners were praying for us and sending cards, bringing over food, giving hugs and dropping by the office to express their concern. This was all derived out of the circle of care that surrounds our community. They would surely be embarrassed that I am even writing about it. While I have been preaching that we need to be a kingdom community, they taught me what it really means. They taught me how to *be* community.

Spiritually, what binds us in this community of faith is our shared baptism. My church traditions have always taught that there is no supernatural change implicit in sacramental acts—baptism is representative of prevenient and saving grace; the Eucharist is a *memorial* to Jesus. This Protestant perspective is dangerous not only because of its metaphysic of nominalism but also because it reduces theology to a flat metaphor. Instead, baptism is the beginning of a journey of change and self-transcendence, culminating in the participation of a community where individual subjectivity is invested in the other in a deeply existential way. This perpetual parthenogenesis of creation, occurring at different levels, between and within the dialectic of life and death, is the meaning of our baptism. Baptism is our invitation into *supernatural intersubjectivity.*

Part 1

I was baptized September 11, 1978. My mother came from the "Weinbrenner" Church of God tradition, a radical revivalist movement with roots upstream on the Susquehanna River from their farm near Bainbridge, Pennsylvania. We attended my father's family church, a product of the "Albright Brethren" movement that was nominally Wesleyan and matter-of-factly evangelical. The little country church, Kinderhook Evangelical

Congregational Church near Columbia, Pennsylvania, even has a stained-glass window in the rear of the sanctuary, facing the road with the name "Rodkey." We were church people.

Despite the evangelical and "moral-majority" beliefs of the congregation, their baptismal theology was Wesleyan, and my grandmother apparently pressured my mother to have me baptized as a young child. The irony of this is that while my mother's Weinbrenner background made her suspicious of infant baptism, my insistent paternal grandmother grew up Mennonite; so Mennonite that they spoke Pennsylvania Dutch in their itinerant-farmer home and she was not baptized until after she was married in her twenties. The double-edged conflict regarding baptism resides at the beginning of my spiritual journey in the church.

When I was about thirteen, there was conflict at church. Apparently words were exchanged among some of the men of the congregation and the pastor between Sunday school and Sunday worship, which led some parents to meet us children at the classroom door, saying, "We're leaving." *Leaving church?* I was ecstatic. We loaded into the station wagon and jumped on the road as my parents started talking. I do not believe they knew where they were going, but then we drove past a big brick United Methodist Church. I had always noticed it when we passed, not only because of its size and location but also because of its fairly modern design and the bricks that were exactly the same color as those of the public schools in my district. My father saw that worship was about to start, so he turned around and went into the parking lot. Dad said, "We're going to church."

Part 2

The date of my Confirmation as a United Methodist had arrived. We were asked individually if we believed in all sorts of things, and my parents laid hands on me. I distinctly remember, for the first time, really questioning my commitment to the church and my beliefs, but my confirmation did not help me learn healthy questioning of faith. Instead, it discouraged me from asking honest questions by failing to provide a context for questioning. I answered the questions "Yes," "I do," and "I will." But I knew I was a liar. In the records of that United Methodist Church, I am probably recorded on that day as a "Confirmation" or a "First profession of faith"; what really happened was my first inward denial of faith.

As I stood and looked out at the congregation with children a couple years younger, some of them with the wetness of their baptism nearly dried, I wondered whether everyone there knew I was a liar and unworthy of the cake they served after the service. I felt like a failure to God, my parents, and my church. The church's act of grace was one that was believed to have confirmed faith, but the process had actually led me to deny faith. Yet the reception I received from the church was a radical welcome, and I figured I could relearn the faith of my childhood, and I could easily hide in the business of spaghetti dinners and volleyball nights with youth at church.

Part 3

I was twenty-one, and December 24, 1998, was a Christmas Eve that I will not forget. I met with the local United Methodist District Superintendent, who offered me his support, and I mailed my seminary applications. I prepared myself for the three Christmas Eve worship services that I attended every year at my home church, in which I played the trumpet with our brass ensemble. In the first service, which was more formal with preaching, Rev. Fowler talked little about Christmas Eve and mostly about how proud he was of the church, and that "you wouldn't believe how many awesome candidates we have for ministry coming out of this congregation." I believed that he was thinking of me. I was really touched that he would say it publicly.

The second service was the children's service, which included a play where one kid acted like he was David Letterman and did a "Top 10" list about Christmas, but then the angel of Christmas past came to get the Letterman character and showed him the *real* meaning of Christmas, namely Jesus. I watched the service at the back of the sanctuary, which was really an auditorium with a cross, and saw a sea of digital lights; this was the year that digital video recording had found its way into the upper-middle class. I began to count how many people were recording the play, and I stopped when I got to around eighty. In some cases, husbands and wives were *both* taping the play with two different camcorders. As this went on, and the kids kept singing schmaltzy songs with a fully orchestrated backing track piped in from a CD, I noticed the professional lighting unit that was being used. The program was too good, and it was meaningless to me.

I began to feel an overwhelming sense of dread, and then the dread turned to nausea. I became physically ill, and I could not play the trumpet for the end of the worship service. I had experienced the *feeling* of the death of God. The angst was Kierkegaardian. While children sang about the importance of "keeping Christ in Christmas," they had essentially escorted Christ out of the building. The last musical number had the kids dressing up in different costumes from around the world, showing the Letterman character that Christmas is celebrated all over the world; every racial and cultural trope became openly exposed. The radical message of Christmas was lost upon a dead and empty Christ celebrated with the tapping feet of children. They were dancing on the grave of God.

I was able to play the trumpet for the third Christmas Eve service, but the *feeling* and *horror* of God's death continued. Rev. Fowler began to talk about the *meaning* of Christmas, but for him the meaning of Christmas is that the answer to the world's problems comes into the world. And—I still remain dumbfounded that he said this—the reason communism is bad is because it has no Christmas, and therefore no Christ; the reason Buddhism has no answers to life's big questions is because Buddhists don't celebrate Christmas, and have no Christ. And so on. And people said "Amen" and waved their hands as if the Holy Spirit had come upon them.

Part 4

I enrolled at the Divinity School of the University of Chicago. I loved Chicago but I disliked my life there. I had little money and did not want to go into irrevocable debt. There were few times that I worked less than three or four jobs; at one point, I actually had six part-time jobs. Luckily, I could study during some of them. Nothing loomed over me more than the fact I was in a very expensive graduate program for a church that, in my estimation, neither liked me nor had a future for me. The homosexuality debate became more heated in the United Methodist Church, and the denomination was becoming increasingly polarized. Every day, it seemed, there was a new story on the Internet about the American Culture Wars working through the diversity of the denomination.

My approval process to be ordained was not only a disaster; it was humiliating and draining. I went to meeting after meeting seeking approval as a candidate for ordination, and I was given a different reason every time for why I would not be approved. We talked about the Bible, my journey, theology, and seminary, but the bottom line was that all they cared about was homosexuality, and if the conversation was not about homosexuality it was really a veiled way about talking about homosexuality. I assume a fear was that if I were ordained, then they were approving a clergy vote that would challenge the *status quo*. A rumor that I was secretly gay began in the congregation and came back to a family member. Another church member took me aside on a Sunday morning and said to me that if I were ordained, the only church to which the Bishop would ever appoint me would be in Germantown, "with all the niggers and queers." Germantown

is the historic northwestern neighborhood of Philadelphia, where, coinci-
dentally, the United Methodist Church would a few years later place one
of their own pastors, Rev. Beth Stroud, on a church trial for being gay. She
would be defrocked in 2005 at the campground I attended as a teen.

During the final meeting with the ordination committee, one
committee member was so frightened of me that she moved her chair when
I came into the room because she did not even want to sit next to me, and
she started praying aloud while I was speaking. I had my transcript from
the University of Chicago to demonstrate that my grades were good and
also to suggest that the ordination process itself was a distraction to my
seminary education, but they decided to pick apart the titles of the courses
and the credentials of the professors. The senior pastor's approval of the
University of Chicago as a valid school for pastoral training came up as an
issue for discussion, and he then admitted that he thought that "University of Chicago" meant I was really attending "Moody Bible Institute."
I laughed and laughed, as if there could not be a bigger difference; but
now it appeared that I had duped everyone regarding where I was going to
school.

At the end of the final meeting, I asked the committee only to consider
an acceptance or a rejection of my ordination application, as they kept
tabling their decision. I would not accept a tabled decision. They made
me leave the room, and after about an hour, the associate pastor came out
to tell me that they would be discussing me late into the night, and it was
already late, so I should go home. I should not have left, but I did. The next
morning the associate pastor called to inform me that my candidacy was
terminated. A few weeks later, I received a letter, signed by my old Sunday
school teacher, explaining that I was not theologically a Christian by their
definition, thus officially rendering me a heretic at age twenty-three.

Nine years later, I returned to that very church on the anniversary of
my ordination in the United Church of Christ, having forgone standing in
the United Methodist Church. It was a weekday afternoon, and I walked
up to the church and opened the doors, which were unlocked. No one
was present. I looked around, sat in the pews, and walked up to the stage
area. I had my copy of Nietzsche's *Gay Science* and read aphorism 124 out
loud. After I realized that the church was empty, I yelled the words of the
madman. The sanctuary's acoustics were too professionally engineered for
any echo. With the madman's final lament—"What are these churches now
but the tombs and sepulchers of God?"—the deadening silence that the
empty pews responded spoke like the strange hum of snowflakes falling

onto the grass. No one was listening, and no one really cared or even noticed. I left the church knowing that I was owed an apology, but also knowing that I would never receive one. But while I continue to try to move on, I also know that I am not quite ready.

Part 5

While I am not ready to move on from the church, the force that keeps pulling me back is the belief that I am not alone in my exile. So much navel-gazing is spent at denominational and local congregational meetings about why young people do not return to the church or why contemporary families do not take advantage of the programs that churches offer, while it is alarmingly clear that the large numbers of people who reject the church are not really welcome there anyway. Their rejection of the church is a proper one; the church left them a long time ago. I have learned to shape my being to live into a ministry that responds to the failure of the church, a failure that has become especially acute over the past fifty years. This is often a lonely walk, but it is one that shows some signs of life on the margins. That said, the threat of denominational death has become an institutional reality to most mainstream churches in the United States, and they now must listen to the younger voices that have chosen an avenue of noncomplacency. So much of the institutional church's history over the past ten years has surrounded the political polarizations of abortion, homosexuality, and local autonomy.

A community of the baptized, when acting ideally, understands baptism within its own structure. If baptism is the fluid that glues our community together, even as its washing sets us apart, a baptism community recognizes that to say "no" to a young adult for dissent from doctrine is at its base a violation of baptismal covenanting. The words said to the newly baptized are often, "Remember your baptism and be faithful." These words are usually said by the ordained to the one who is wet, from the individual representing the brokenness of the church to the one to whom God is saying through baptism, "You are whole, and you are loved." The exhortation of remembering requires institutional memory and recognition of brokenness: the community remembers their own baptismal covenants through the bestowal of the sacrament and its promises. The litany implies recognition of the church's imperfection, and baptism demands transcendence beyond its own flaws, as much as is possible.

The image I have of baptism, which is perhaps a caricature, is a community gathered on the muddy riverbank singing "Shall We Gather at the River?" To stand as the worshiping community as baptismal witness is a dirty, messy affair, both joyful and humbling. Baptism is also a metaphor for our dependence on water, not only in the physical makeup of our bodies but also for our nourishment. To the words "Remember your baptism and be faithful," I recall the words of Luce Irigaray: "So remember the liquid ground. And taste the saliva in your mouth also. . . . Or again: how you stop speaking when you drink. And how necessary all of that is for you!" Being a congregational witness to baptism reifies the brokenness of our community and our reliance on the sacrament to hold us together and keep us accountable. It connects us to the elements and challenges us toward self-transcendence. "These fluids softly mark the time. And there is no need to knock, just listen to hear the music. With very small ears."[48]

On the margin of the river, washing up its silver spray, we will walk and worship ever, all the happy golden day. Yes, we'll gather by the river . . . that flows by the throne of God.[49]

CHRISTOPHER D. RODKEY is the Pastor of St. Paul's United Church of Christ in Dallastown, Pennsylvania. He also teaches at Penn State York, of The Pennsylvania State University, and at Lexington Theological Seminary. He holds the PhD in Philosophy and Theology and Master of Philosophy from Drew University, the DMin in Pastoral Ministry from Meadville Lombard Theological School, the MDiv from the University of Chicago Divinity School, and a BA in Philosophy and English from Saint Vincent College. He is the author of *Too Good to be True: Radical Christ Preaching, Year A* (Christian Alternative, 2014) and *The Synoptic Gospel: Teaching the Brain to Worship* (University Press of America, 2012). An occasional blogger for "An und fur sich" (www.itself.wordpress.com), he lives with his wife and four children.

20

Preaching with the Enemy

Julie Faith Parker

I remember sitting in a darkened movie theater watching the preview and thinking, "I will never see this movie." The year was 1990, and the trailer for *Sleeping with the Enemy*, starring Julia Roberts, showed a woman living in a private hell. Her controlling husband abuses her and she tries to fake her own death in an effort to escape. It looked tense and scary, just the kind of movie I loathe. But the film also felt eerily familiar, even though I have never been domestically abused and was just happily married. I recognized the feeling of being unsafe in a relationship with a controlling man because I was preaching with the enemy.

I had graduated from Union Theological Seminary in New York City two years earlier and been ordained in the United Methodist Church; I was excited about ministry. My father, sister, and new husband were all ordained. Having grown up in the church, I realized that being a pastor was impossibly demanding work. I had witnessed all that my father went through: the crazy hours, the incessant needs of parishioners, the weekends that never felt like weekends, and, worst of all, the few toxic folks in nearly every congregation who tried to poison the whole church—and sometimes succeeded. Knowing this and having completed my seminary training, I felt reasonably ready for a pastoral position.

Still, I was nervous about some aspects of the job that I knew nothing about: finance and administration. To serve as an associate pastor seemed like the perfect solution since I could learn more about these responsibilities while serving a church. My sister was also an associate pastor at the time and loved it. In the United Methodist system, the bishop appoints the minister to a charge (position); I requested and received an appointment as an associate pastor. I was happy about the job and eager to begin work. Little did I realize that this was the start of my professional nightmare.

When I received my appointment, I quickly heard about the senior pastor with whom I would be working. Let's call him "Joe." A lifelong pastor, Joe was in his mid-fifties and wore dark-rimmed bifocals. He was balding and a little bent over, yet very strong in body and will. Joe had a reputation as an isolationist. He did not participate in (and indeed, I discovered later, proudly eschewed) any committees or activities of the conference (the association of churches in a particular area, in UM parlance). Instead, he ran his church with great pride and efficiency. Joe believed, as many perfectionists do, that something done right was something done his way.

By him.

He acted as the church sexton, polishing floors, changing the signboard out front, regulating the heating system, etc. He functioned as the church treasurer, officially giving this title to a docile woman in her eighties who penned every check according to his exact specifications (even though this simple task was hard for her). He wrote and produced the church newsletter, fancying himself as an ecclesiastical Garrison Keillor, and seemed somewhat dismayed that no book contract had come his way to publish his assembled columns. Joe was the man in charge; things were done his way or no way. He had been at the church for sixteen years when I got there, and anyone who did not like his style was long gone. To Joe's credit, the church was a well-oiled machine, but just because something (or someone) is functioning does not mean it (or they) is healthy.

Other clergy, especially women, warned me. The previous associate pastor, a woman whom I'll call "Miriam," had been called to ministry after a career in teaching. She went to seminary for many years part-time at night, got ordained, and had been genuinely enthusiastic when she began working with Joe. Before I took on the job she had just vacated, I sought Miriam out and arranged a time to have coffee. Our conversation felt like a pastoral counseling session. She was deeply wounded. Miriam told me how Joe had been publicly dismissive of her to the point where she came to doubt the call that had propelled her through so many years of sacrifice and study. Miriam's husband, Bob, had recently retired, enabling them to move into the community of this church. Bob was a skilled carpenter and noticed that the Sunday school children had worship each week in a space with no altar. He built an altar for the children so they could assemble around it for prayer and Bible readings. It was stunning—buttery oak wood with swirls of grain lovingly polished to a smooth glow, custom made and beautifully designed for that room. Bob poured weeks into this labor of love and installed it in its proper place.

Joe never said a word about the altar to the congregation. No announcement during a worship service. No recognition in the bulletin. No "thank you" spoken in passing. Not a single line in Joe's precious newsletter uttered a phrase of thanks. Bob was struggling to feel useful in his retirement and in his new role as a clergy spouse. Joe insulted Bob firmly and silently by pointedly ignoring his offering. "I can forgive Joe for what he did to me," Miriam confided, tears welling in her eyes, "but I'll *never* forgive him for what he did to my husband."

Pastoral ministry with Joe had scarred Miriam, but it still didn't scare me. Call it reckless naïveté, unbridled optimism, or just plain stupidity, but I thought, "Not to worry. I can do this." Worse, maybe I had a touch of hubris. I had been a strong student in seminary—won awards even—and figured I was bright enough to work it out. I would get to that church, pour myself into my responsibilities, and show Joe my capability. The scene in *The Sound of Music* came to mind where Julie Andrews, playing the erstwhile Sister Maria, takes the bus to meet Captain von Trapp and the children for the first time. While singing in perfect pitch, Maria positively *exudes* confidence, and look what happened there: she was fabulous at her job and the imposing man never got the best of *her*! That was my strategy: "They'll have to agree I have confidence in me!"

And so, like my singing heroine, I went to a new place to start a new job. Perhaps the day I moved to that town should have tipped me off. Over the phone I had told Joe the date when I would be moving into the associate pastor's parsonage. My then-fiancé, Bill, helped me load the truck to take my belongings to the house that would first be mine and then, when we married in a few weeks, our new home together. Joe had said that folks from the congregation would meet us at the house to help us unload the truck. I was grateful for the offer of help.

We drove the U-Haul to the parsonage address at 10 a.m. on Wednesday, July 2, exactly when we had said we would arrive. No one was there, and the house was locked. Somewhat baffled, I walked to the church next door, found Joe, and asked for a key to the house. He explained that folks from the church had been there *the day before*, waiting for us with trays of cookies, pitchers of lemonade, and hands eager to help. "You said you'd arrive on Tuesday, July 1, but today is Wednesday, July 2. Everyone was here yesterday," he remarked with a slightly disdainful tone.

It had been clear to me for weeks exactly which day I was moving. Why would I have given the wrong day? And even if I had given a confused date, why didn't Joe call me to clarify? I started to realize that this was his way:

deduce, decide, do. My parents did not live far away, so I called them and they came over to help unload the truck. Joe helped too.

While we were lugging boxes into the dining room, my mother asked me, "So how was your drive with the U-Haul?"

"Oh, it was okay," I told her, "but I feel bad. People from the congregation were here *yesterday* to help us; they thought we were coming then."

Joe emerged from the kitchen to snap at me, "Julie, you've got help now. It all worked out fine." Once again, I thought what I did not dare utter: "I'm not your daughter, and I wasn't talking to you."

Joe and I would come to perfect these rounds of silently warped communication. In the beginning, it wasn't so bad. I was excited about the job and threw myself into it. My responsibilities were typical for an associate pastor at a 500-member church. Every Sunday I was up in the chancel assisting in leading worship, and I preached once a month. I ran the youth group, taught Sunday school, and led the youth retreats. Church visitation was part of my routine, and I went to see those who were homebound or in the hospital. My week was peppered with other facets of church life: singing in the choir, joining in fellowship activities, teaching a Bible study, and attending church meetings. On the surface, it seemed fine.

But under this veneer of pastoral tranquility, tension was growing. Joe did not talk *with* me or *to* me; he talked *at* me. Meetings, I came to discover, were not for discussing ideas. They were gatherings where groups of congregants assembled to put their rubber stamp of approval on what Joe had already decided. So perhaps it was foolish of me to suggest an idea at a meeting, not to mention one that I knew Joe did not like.

Our big blowout erupted over a tiny issue: Christmas bulbs. I thought it would be enjoyable and eye opening for the youth to take a trip to Washington, DC; I had lived there the year before and had lots of contacts with people doing exciting urban ministry. The teenagers could experience the nation's capital, grow in faith, and have fun together. To fund the trip, we could sell Christmas bulbs with a picture of the church on them. An artist in the church was glad to do the drawing. There was a company where we could order the custom-made shiny bulbs. Families had been in this church for generations, and I knew they would buy these special ornaments to support the youth. I was enthused and told Joe about my idea.

"No," he said, "I don't like it. Too much hassle." He paused, then continued, "Here's my advice to you: hide your light under a bushel."

That knocked the wind right out of me. Did I hear him correctly, verbatim countering the gospel? I silently got up and left his office. That was supposed to be the end of that.

Maybe it was my desire to show him that my light was going to shine. For whatever reason (naïveté? optimism? stupidity? . . . hubris?), I had the audacity to bring up my idea at a committee meeting.

"Any other business?" Joe perfunctorily asked when the meeting was essentially over.

"Actually," I ventured, "I wondered if I could have a few minutes to discuss a fundraiser for the youth."

Joe glared at me, but I continued and explained my idea. When I was done, Joe could not contain his rage. He was seething. "Julie," he reprimanded, "I told you that I didn't like that idea."

"I just thought it was something we could discuss," I courageously continued.

Ed, an older man in the congregation—a little stout, stooped over, no neck—got red in the face and said, "Damn you, Julie, be quiet."

Whoa . . . cursed at in a church meeting for sharing an idea to benefit the teenagers; this was a new nadir.

I went home and drank two beers. My husband, a kind soul who has had his nose broken in a street fight because he's so feisty, was livid. Every molecule in his being wanted to go two doors over to Joe's house and punch him in the face. He was pained to see me like this. Generally, I'm a pretty happy person, but here I was, a newlywed madly in love with my husband, yet I cried nearly every night. Fortunately, though, I had my family around me who understood ministry. I had friends who supported me. Because of them, I knew that the root of this problem was not my ineptitude.

Yes, I had a lot to learn, but something was seriously wrong here that was beyond my control. But what to do?

I sought help in the church hierarchy. First, I set up an appointment with the supervising minister for my district, who is called a district superintendent in United Methodist polity. I went to his office and told him of my experiences, struggling vainly not to cry (again). His response? To hold me tight in long hugs. I was a young woman in my twenties; he was a middle-aged man in his forties. I felt uncomfortable. Today this would be recognized as sexual harassment. Then, I just knew that he was not going to help me, so I moved on.

I shared my story with the clergywomen's group. They listened, prayed, and cared. Their response validated my situation but didn't ameliorate it.

I went to the bishop. He was a busy man, and I specifically remember that our meeting had to be rescheduled five times. Finally, his assistant told me that he was going to be at a conference in the United Nations building on the east side of Manhattan. I could go to a specific room in the UN, and he would leave the meeting to talk to me. So that's what I did.

I got to the UN, went through all the security, and made my way up to the designated room. I stood at the open door; the bishop saw me, excused himself, and came out to talk with me. I shared my story yet again, fighting back the tears. When I was done, maybe ten minutes later, the bishop asked me, "What's the effect on the laity?"

Good for him. This bishop cared about the congregation. I told him that they felt caught. They didn't want conflict, and neither did I. He asked how he could help, and I told him that I wanted to stay at the church for one more year. In the United Methodist Church back then, a pastor who served two years full-time in a congregation would be ordained an Elder. This meant you would have a guaranteed appointment if you ever needed one. I wanted that security and was willing to do what was necessary to get it. The bishop gave his word that he would support me in my decision to stay there another year.[50] With the bishop's blessing, I followed through on that plan.

My professional relationship with Joe went from chilly to icy détente. Every week we said just *two words* to each other. We both sang in the church choir. On Sunday mornings at 9 a.m., I would see Joe in the rehearsal room and say "Good morning" or, if I were in generous mood, "Good morning, Joe." His response: "Good morning" (no "Julie" added). We were both pastoring the same church, and that was the full extent of our speaking to each other for a year. But we had to communicate more than this to function, so we spoke to each other through our sermons. He would preach about listening, growing, and learning from those with experience. I would preach about kindness, compassion, and letting your light shine. It would have been comical if it weren't so sad.

At the end of the second year, I left that church. There was an awkward send-off coffee hour, and Joe was conspicuously absent. Bill and I moved to another town where he had begun serving as the congregational minister. Looking back, I still remember my two years as an associate pastor as a painful time, although my own scars have now largely healed. I am glad that I extricated myself strategically. I also left the pastoral ministry, went on to campus ministry, spent years as a PhD student, and now am a professor of Old Testament. Had I been in a successful first pastorate, I might not have taken this route. I might be a pastor instead of a professor. I have come to believe that being a professor is my true calling, however. Perhaps that's a gift Joe unintentionally gave me.

But there's another gift he gave me on purpose. Along with controlling everything else, Joe controlled my salary. Without consulting me in any way, he put the maximum amount in my pension account. Now, over twenty years later, this has amounted to something. Nothing I could retire on, but certainly more than I would have had I been given any options about pension contributions myself. So my difficult story of preaching with the enemy ends on a note of grace.

And that is the name of the church that Joe and I once served together: Grace.

JULIE FAITH PARKER has a PhD with distinction in Old Testament/Hebrew Bible from Yale University, and is Assistant Professor of Old Testament at Trinity Lutheran Seminary in Columbus, Ohio. She has also taught at Yale University, Andover Newton Theological School, Fordman University, and New York Theological Seminary (teaching inmates at Sing Sing Correctional Facility). She is the author of five books and numerous articles. Her most recent book, *Valuable and Vulnerable*, is about children in the Hebrew Bible and was published by Brown University (2013). Her earlier books address topics of clergywomen, homelessness, teen ethics, and leadership. An Elder in the United Methodist Church, she continues to preach and teach as an invited speaker. She and her husband, Rev. Dr. Bill Crawford, have been married twenty-six years and are the proud parents of two grown children: a son, Graham, and a daughter, Mari.

21

Lions and Bears and Education for Ministry

John M. Imbler

Note: This essay was originally an address I delivered in January 1994, once in Enid and once in Tulsa, Oklahoma. The occasions were my installation as vice president for administration, assistant professor of practical theology, director of Disciples of Christ ministerial formation, and director of supervised ministries on the Enid campus of Phillips Theological Seminary. The intent was to introduce my perspectives on ministry and ministerial education to the whole seminary community as well as to challenge students to think broadly as they engaged their studies—that is, beyond merely achieving a grade. The address was reprised as a sermon for opening chapel in Tulsa September 2008 upon my return from a sabbatical leave. Emendations reflect my learning over those fourteen years plus more for this publication. I've discovered over twenty years of teaching that although churches have appropriated their understandings of ministry differently and modes of education have changed, these core values remain the same.

In his 1967 inaugural address at the fall convocation at Vanderbilt University Divinity School in Nashville, Tennessee, incoming dean Walter J. Harrelson, a Hebrew Bible scholar, read selected verses from the seventeenth chapter of 1 Samuel, then made the following observation: "It's dangerous being a shepherd—one has to contend with lions and bears—and the call of the Lord" (1 Sam 17:32-37). There are inherent hazards in shepherding. Today's lions and bears appear in the forms of church boards, bishops, regional and conference ministers, candidacy committees, field education supervisors, deans, faculty, and a host of others who seemingly sneak toward the flock threatening those things under our care, indeed, threatening us—our beliefs, our preconceptions, and sometimes the very foundations of our faith.

Like David who was blessed by Saul then involuntarily girded with heavy armor and weapons, we first feel blessed by our calls but soon become burdened by the weight of uncomfortable, ill-fitting restrictions, rules, and expectations that impede us doing what we know we're capable of doing. Our faith is grounded, we feel secure in our calls, and we seem to have a clear sense of who we are and where we want to go. Ah, but the lions and bears await. Ministerial candidates are faced with ordination requirements or other forms of professional certification. Ministers perhaps are seeking a pastoral call or waiting for a church appointment. For teachers, it's living under the rules of tenure or negotiating with a publisher or contending with an editor. We throw off the cumbersome heavy armor and lay down the oversized weapons to pick up a sling—with which we've developed some proficiency—and a handful of carefully selected stones to use as projectiles. We are now more agile, can move more quickly, can hide behind a bush more easily. We have developed coping mechanisms that have served us well and adequately protect us against dangers.

The shepherd image is a warm, idyllic one, presenting to our minds a truly pastoral scene. But our flocks, whether in the pew or the meeting room, are not sheep that can be herded from one grassy hill to the next; they're human beings with wills and opinions that may well differ from our own. As ministers of the gospel or leaders in the church and society, in order to serve effectively we need to be empowered by the Holy Spirit and equipped with the best tools available to do the tasks to which we are called. Weapons are used to destroy, and tools are used to create. Regardless of the many warrior references found in the Hebrew Scriptures and the Epistles and even the church's hymnody, it's long past time for Christians to lay down the arms of battle and pick up the tools for building.

Education is one of those critical tools. In his chapter of *Good Steward-ship*, former ATS director William Baumgartner wrote, "The theological school alone bears the responsibility for not only academic teaching, but also for the practical professional training and spiritual maturation of students."[51] Baumgartner correctly identifies the components of a solid ministerial education program, but his locus is misstated. Clearly no other institution is as well positioned to do this complex task because proper theological education consists of both academic learning and ministerial formation. With the seminary rooted in both the academy and the church, it is uniquely able to connect intellectual growth with spiritual development and the art and practices of ministry. Academic teaching, practical professional training, and spiritual maturation each has its own integrity, but when any one of the three is absent or devalued, the mission of the seminary is debased. Concurrently, when attention to church is neglected, the purpose of the seminary is violated.

During his twelve-year tenure, the academic dean at Phillips Theological Seminary repeated the same personal story at every new student orientation. When he left home to enter seminary, the charge given by people in his sending church was not to let seminary change him. "Come back the same as you are," they said. Many of us in ministry have heard that charge: don't let seminary change you. If it's doing its job properly, though, seminary will change a person, and the reality is that even those of us who teach in seminary regularly experience growth, encounter change, and gain new perspectives. Actually, isn't that a mission of the church, to embrace and promote change? Isn't that a function of ministry, to be on the leading edge? Isn't that what the Scriptures call us to do? The seminary—literally meaning a seedbed or nursery—is a place of planting and nurture. In addition to imparting a specific corpus of knowledge, it is called to impart skills of interpreting, practices of understanding, and ways of knowing. It seeks to instill new disciplines of learning—learning that must not cease when a paper is turned in, when a final exam is taken, or, especially, when a diploma is received. A sad indictment of too many clergy is that their professional libraries do not expand after their graduations. One role of the seminary is to establish a pattern for learning that is engaged for a lifetime in any place a minister lives, works, and worships.

In a newsletter from a local church in Tulsa, the senior pastor wrote in his weekly column, "When I completed my first course in college I learned that my well-informed and challenging history teacher continued to read hundreds of books after finishing graduate school." He went on, "Even the most advanced masters require practice and new challenges."[52] And this pastor lives that out in his ministry.

But the seminary does not stand alone in this educational/formational enterprise, nor should it want to. The church, too, is a teacher—surely in congregations but also in judicatories, agencies, and in whatever configurations a faith community organizes and expresses itself. At a board meeting in a congregation I attended some years ago, the name of an entering seminarian was presented for consideration to fill the part-time position of director of Christian education. He was inexperienced in ministry, there was only a sketchy job description, and incredibly that particular seminary at the time had no supervisory requirements for field education. I gave what some might have regarded as an impassioned speech on the need for nurture and guidance of ministerial candidates, insisting that if the congregation was merely looking for an extra pair of hands to do the work no one else wanted to do—at a cheap price I might add—it would likely be disappointed. In addition was the real prospect of dooming that particular program to failure and possibly dissuading that individual from pursuing full-time ministry. There needs to be clarity, goals, and accountability. Driving home after the meeting, my wife perceptively asked how many more churches would be subjected to that speech. I've lost count.

I do not like the term "student ministers" any more than I like the term "junior deacons." It's descriptive to be sure, but seminarians are ministers who concurrently are students and vice versa. The worth of integrative education within the school cannot be overstated, but for the health of ministry, integrative approaches within the church must also be undertaken. We are always in training regardless of experience and age. This is where Baumgartner misstates the locus. The sole responsibility for the preparation for vital ministry is neither the seminary's nor the church's but rather rests on both together, however disproportionately those may be exercised at times. And the caution of lions and bears here is to make sure that neither attacks or undermines the other. Approaches to theological education and ministerial formation in the United States have undergone notable changes over the past 300 years as religion and society, working both in concert and at odds, have weathered significant transition periods. Responsible ministry requires a constant state of learning, adaptation, and reflection.

The third partner in ministerial education is the learner. Regardless of how well a curriculum is designed or how person-friendly an ecclesial process is or how supportive a congregation may be, neither the seminary nor the church can make ministers. This is the province of God. The critical mission of institutions is to enable those who have been called to prepare for their callings. In reality it's not the lions or bears or boards or bishops that make being a shepherd dangerous. Dean Harrelson was correct: it's how the call of the Lord affects us.

In what I consider a timeless work, H. Richard Niebuhr identifies four types of call:

(1) *The call to be a Christian*, which is variously described as the call to the discipleship of Jesus Christ, to hearing and doing the Word of God . . . . (2) *The secret call*, that inner persuasion . . . whereby a person feels summoned by God to take up the work of ministry. . . . (3) *The providential call* . . . which comes through the equipment of a person . . . for the exercise of the office. That is, preparation, education, and practice in both formal and informal ways . . . . (4) *The ecclesiastical call*, that is the invitation extended by some community or institution of the Church to engage in the work of ministry.[53]

That is the process of certification by the church and call or appointment to a ministerial position. Combined into a unit, these four calls express vocation—*vocare*—in its purest meaning.

Seminarians bring a wealth of experiences and education to their theological studies, having lived and led in a variety of vocational and avocational arenas. Those experiences and educations are not to be discarded but rather included in the dialogues throughout their courses. In this regard, it is incumbent on all to listen with courtesy—but not without critique—to what each person has to say. And that is the same within the church. For continuing education many years back, I took a course on prophets with Walter Brueggemann. Regardless of the topic, he always devoted a few minutes at the end of each class session to ask, "How does this inform your ministry?" This has become a mantra for me that I ask my students over and over. Moreover, how does an issue, idea, or a new interpretation open our minds so that our ministries are continually formed? Is this not dangerous? Opening our minds is tantamount to exposing our souls. Responding to the call of God is risky because it forces us to face ourselves—our weaknesses, our doubts, our fears. Ministerial education presses us to test our patterns of thinking, challenge our assumptions, and redefine our language.

Another risk is that of coming to terms with new terms. It's not unusual to hear laity comment that their preacher had never told them something that was revelatory, exciting, or mind changing such as a new theological concept or a different way to read a biblical text. Theological education is not a matter of learning; it's also a matter of transmitting what has been learned in ways that are appropriate and helpful. Our seminary president constantly reminds us that Jesus deserves an educated church. The armor and weapons of Saul are not needed, and the sling and stones of David must be discarded. Preparation for and growth in ministry is not a contest that determines winners and losers. Far too many church bodies expect that a graduating seminarian is a finished product. Students often assume that a theological professor has all the answers to complex faith questions. Spiritual and intellectual maturity is a process—a journey—to be enjoyed but never fully completed. At a seminary graduation, upon conferring degrees one president commented that the students had now mastered divinity. At no time should clergy be so bold as to assume such mastery. At the same time, both church and seminary have every right to expect high quality and deep commitment in ministers and students.

The lions and bears of the church should not be feared or destroyed, although approaching them warily is advised. The assurance in facing the risks, the dangers, the lions and the bears is that God doesn't call us without equipping us. Our job is not protection; it's discernment, to understand God truly using all the tools at our disposal. It's one thing to hear the call of the Lord; it's another to act on that call faithfully even in the face of dangers.

JOHN M. IMBLER is ordained in the Christian Church (Disciples of Christ) and married with three adult children and six grandchildren. He has served as the Stephen J. England Associate Professor of the History of Christianity and Disciples Studies at Phillips Theological Seminary in Tulsa, Oklahoma. He has been awarded the Doctor of Divinity from Columbia College, and holds the DMin from Phillips Theological Seminary, Master of Sacred Theology and the MDiv from Christian Theological Seminary, and a BA from Butler University. Some of his notable publications are *Discerning the Call: Advancing the Quality of Ordained Leadership* (Chalice, 1992), *Beyond Buffalo: Alexander Campbell on Education for Ministry* (Disciples of Christ Historical Society, 1992), *A Passion for Christian Unity: Essays in Honor of William Tabbernee* (Chalice, 2009). Having retired from full-time teaching in 2014, he enjoys reading, fishing, and golf.

A Final Word

A work like this is an intense labor of love. Finding people to submit personal stories about the hardships of vocational ministry wasn't easy by any stretch of the imagination. Almost unanimously, those who learned about what I was looking to do expressed a personal and professional sigh of relief that such an important topic would finally be addressed. Many colleagues were eager to be involved somehow. Others, however, while noting the need for such a resource, chose against participating because it was deemed potentially too provocative or risky. I have learned, and the Bible surely attests, that when you begin telling the truth in light of who God is, singing "Kumbaya" usually isn't quick to follow. Complications are actually more probable—yes, even in and maybe especially in Christian circles. We just aren't good with discussing truth partly because wading through its magnitude makes us uncomfortable. We are scared of confronting what life has been and what it is in order to pursue life for how it *should* be from God's perspective. I am sad to say that the church sucks at conflict.

For example, same-sex marriage and LGBT[54] affirmation are issues that we struggle to discuss constructively these days. I believe this has a lot to do with how the issues have been politicized in private and public arenas. Nevertheless, it isn't going away anytime soon, especially with the Supreme Court's recent ruling—and neither is the issue of women in ministry. Although now more than ever the gifts and graces of women are being recognized through ordination and leadership in church-related vocations, there is still more work to be done. The way I see it, many personalities exist in the Christian household of faith. Our family reunions are messy, full of intoxicated cousins twice removed asking for money, adult siblings giving one another the silent treatment, squabbling children, crabby aunts, and crass uncles. We are the same yet so different. Represented in this book are pastors of various perspectives, from the left and right to the middle on any issue under the sun. That level of diversity frightens many people. I just happen not to be one of them.

As a theologically moderate pastor and evangelical, I passionately believe that *all* Christians ought to work out their own salvation with fear and trembling (Phil 2:12) in community, wrestling with what we, by faith, discern as God's demands of us. Ephesians 4:4-6 reminds us, "There is one body and one Spirit, just as you were called to the one hope of your calling, one Lord, one baptism, one God and Father of all, who is above all and through all and in all." In this sense, being conversant and in relationship with those from different Christian tribes can be a beautiful experience. In his landmark text *The Humanity of God*, theologian Karl Barth wrote,

> A free theologian works in communication with other theologians. . . .
> He waits for them and asks them to wait for him. Our sadly lacking yet
> indispensable theological co-operation depends directly or indirectly on
> whether or not we are willing to wait for one another, perhaps lamenting,
> yet smiling with tears in our eyes.[55]

I believe Jesus is the hope of the world, having been sent so that whoever believes in him shall not perish but have eternal life, for God did not send Jesus into the world to condemn the world, but to save the world through him (John 3:16-17). As he is "the way, and the truth, and the life," we are reconciled to God exclusively through Jesus (John 14:6). Even so, I stand as a peacemaker in mature dialogue with those whose soteriology differs from mine and whose convictions otherwise aren't my own. *Tell the Truth, Shame the Devil: Stories about the Challenges of Young Pastors* is about giving young pastors a vehicle to share their struggles with the world. I pray that God uses it to help lift the veil of secrecy and untruth from vocational ministry, and from Christianity more broadly.

Cowards and champions, manipulators and martyrs can be found among shepherds and sheep alike. There are those whose steady diet of spiritual Similac stunts their growth, as they ought to have already gradu-ated to solid food like meat or tofu (Heb 5:12-14). There are women and men trudging through the gray muck and mire of life, some ruled by fear, some ruled by faith, and some in love with their own shadow. Given what has been shared in this collection, many of us should be pessimistic cynics, frustrated beyond belief, or maybe even heretics whose pain turned into searing hate. But by God's grace that is not anyone's story as best as I know.

We are free indeed (John 8:36) and choose to live, work, and play in light of that truth. We are hopeful in the One who is hope to use us and this book to help transform the world. The late, great R&B crooner Sam Cooke said it well: "It's been a long time coming, but I know a change gon' come." May the Lord Almighty change us all as we seek to be agents of change in his name.

Warmest regards,
James Ellis III

Afterword

Eldon Fry

When James asked me to pen this closing commentary, I shuddered. Not because I dislike writing authentically (for I really do enjoy candid conversation), but like Jack Nicholson's character famously said in *A Few Good Men*, "I don't think you can handle the truth." This was my personal concern. I feared that the memories of an aging pastor might be too intense for someone to read and process. In particular, I did not want to discourage anyone from responding to God's calling in his or her life. I write as someone who began pastoral ministry in college and was later ordained before age twenty-five. I have served in a country town of less than fifty residents, in university towns with great diversity, and on college campuses, as well as serving as a resource for pastors and spouses in difficulty through toll-free phone lines, other organizations (two of which I founded), and retreats. I know all too well how compelling and heartbreaking ministry often is. The stories in *Tell the Truth, Shame the Devil* ring true with what I have heard, experienced, and observed through a lifetime of ministry.

It is not easy for a young pastor to respond to Paul's admonition to "not despise your youth" (1 Tim 4:12; Titus 2:15) when your youthfulness is dismissed or placed at the bottom of what seems to be a giant pyramid scheme. The treatment of young pastors has a shameful track record. Here you have read real stories that are painful and confusing. Many note positive experiences mixed with abusive events. That leaves young pastors in a spiritual dilemma. How can they minister to the very people who have deeply hurt and betrayed them?

I was fortunate to have the beginnings of gray hair at nineteen, so I passed for older and therefore wiser in the eyes of some—more than many young pastors. At the age of nineteen, unlike some young pastors, I married a woman also called to pastoral ministry. Although I do not recommend that as a model, it helped some accept me as an adult. But marriage, white hair, or even my education did not prepare me for the clash of wills with a "church boss/benefactor" whom I would encounter. No one talked about abusive relationships within congregations. No one mentioned the dirty little secrets embedded in churches and covered with years of animosity and pain.

Like some of this book's authors, I was fortunate to survive the church growth movement where worthiness was equated with numerical growth, fortunate to pastor growing churches, so I avoided the pain of being seen as unworthy in that respect. Nevertheless, I have spent significant amounts of time sitting across the table from broken colleagues who questioned their calling and were dealing with disillusionment and depression, having labeled themselves failures because of not experiencing congregational growth. At one point, I pastored a church attended by seven former pastors who had left their congregations filled with pain. One man would not lift his head in the congregation for weeks until healing came.

At another point in my life, I had the privilege of answering a toll-free phone line for pastors, and for their spouses and children who were in trouble. I cannot begin to relate the horror stories and the desperation of those calls. In three years, the amount of monthly calls nearly tripled. Upon hearing the pain, I felt like I needed to take a mental and spiritual bath each day after prayerfully caring for the callers. Fortunately, there are ministries that offer care in that respect these days, many of them led by people who have left ministry due to burnout and/or pain. Even so, these resources can only do so much. They have their limitations in moments of pastoral crisis.

A common theme in *Tell the Truth, Shame the Devil* seems to be deceptive practices by search committees and church boards. Sadly, this is altogether too common. I have experienced it too "firsthand." Arriving at a church for the first time can be disillusioning. It speaks to the spiritual grit of young pastors that they have tried to stay and face the giant of discouragement as they work through their particular reality. Research indicates that we think higher of ourselves than our capabilities allow for, so some of this may be a function of humanity trying to think the best of their church. But as mentioned in the book, some churches simply defend their untruths, and that seems to go beyond human frailty.

I would like to call all of us who love the church to pray for its leadership and for increased integrity and accountability in denominations and within resources of general support that can encourage young pastors, giving oversight to an ethical process for raising new leaders. I encourage young pastors to develop relationships of support with other colleagues rather than competing with them. Opportunities for mentoring relationships might exist among seminary professors, denominational leaders, other pastors, or classmates. I also hope that seminaries and Bible colleges invest the necessary time to encourage future pastors in understanding the importance of these relationships, teaching them how to establish and maintain them. Finally, I pray that more of us, myself included, step up to provide various opportunities to support young pastors. This inevitably will need to take many different forms and shapes based on the giftedness and calling of each of us. I pray that the stories in *Tell the Truth, Shame the Devil* challenge us to action; that like the aging apostle Paul we would invest in young pastors like Timothy, Titus, John Mark, and many others.

ELDON FRY is the Founder and Director of Open Hands in Carlisle, Pennsylvania, having recently retired as the College Pastor at Messiah College. Ordained in the Wesleyan Church, he holds the DMin from the Graduate Theological Foundation, MS in Family Life Education from Kansas State University, and BA in Religion from Oklahoma Wesleyan University.

Notes

1. Eugene H. Peterson, *The Jesus Way: A Conversation on the Way That Jesus Is the Way* (Grand Rapids MI: Wm. B. Eerdmans, 2011) 230.

2. David Kinnaman, *You Lost Me: Why Young Christians are Leaving Church and Rethinking Faith* (Grand Rapids MI: Baker, 2011) 22.

3. Ibid., 32.

4. Ibid, 35, italics original.

5. For more see Ashley-Anne Masters and Stacy Smith, *Bless Her Heart: Life as a Young Clergy Woman* (St. Louis MO: Chalice, 2011).

6. Robert Wuthnow, *After the Baby Boomers: How Twenty- and Thirty-Somethings Are Shaping the Future of American Religion* (Princeton NJ: Princeton University, 2007) 2.

7. King himself has reflected very little on his time at Dexter Avenue Baptist Church. Even his autobiography (Clayborne Carson, ed., *The Autobiography of Martin Luther King, Jr.* [New York: Warner, 1998] 40–49) moves swiftly from his education to the Montgomery Bus Boycott. His own reflections on the beginning of his pastorate at Dexter Avenue would have been an asset for future church leaders.

8. King, in Carson, ed., *Autobiography*, 6, 15.

9. See J.Kwest, www.jkwest.com (the author's website describing his music career).

10. Ronald A. Heifetz and Marty Linsky, *Leadership on the Line: Staying Alive through the Dangers of Leading* (Boston: Harvard Business School, 2002) 51–75.

11. *Martin Luther King Jr. as Pastor*, PBS, http://www.pbs.org/wnet/ religionandethics/episodes/january-13-2006/martin-luther-king-jr-as-pastor/1788/. (The "34-point plan" is not known to exist in its original form, though it is spoken of enough to be larger than anecdote.) King's father was a pastor, as were his grandfather and great-grandfather. Cultural and familial pressures are under-cited in this essay, the focus instead turning to the interplay between congregations and new leaders. We should not underestimate the forces of family or culture in this analysis.

12. Willy G. Vaughn, ed., *Reflections on our Pastor: Dr. Martin Luther King, Jr. at Dexter Avenue Baptist Church, 1954–1960* (Dover MA: Majority, 1999) 22.

13. The term "myth of leadership" borrows from the title of Jeffrey Nielsen's book bearing the same name: *The Myth of Leadership: Creating Leaderless Organizations* (Palo Alto CA: Davies-Black, 2004). Nielsen is a leadership guru and philosopher whose ideas question the existence of any leadership at all, ultimately saying that organizations should be leaderless (that is a caricature of the "peer principle," described at length in his book). I am not making this argument in any form; rather, I am interested in how archetypes of "leader" are formed similarly to those of "hero," "savior," and the like, and how new leaders follow these archetypes.

14. Sharon Parks, *Leadership Can Be Taught* (Boston: Harvard Business School, 2005).

15. Matthew 22:36-40—"Teacher, which commandment in the law is the greatest?" He said to him, "'You shall love the Lord your God with all your heart, and with all your soul, and with all your mind.' This is the greatest and first commandment. And a second is like it: 'You shall love your neighbor as yourself.' On these two commandments hang all the law and the prophets."

16. John 14:12—"Very truly, I tell you, the one who believes in me will also do the works that I do and, in fact, will do greater works than these, because I am going to the Father."

17. In an interview with *Christianity Today* (49/3, March 2005), Eugene Peterson said, "Jesus is the Truth and the Life, but first he's the Way. We can't do Jesus' work in the Devil's way."

18. John Dalberg Acton, *Essays on Freedom and Power* (Boston: Beacon, 1949) 364.

19. See George Button Thompson, *How to Get Along With Your Church: Creating Cultural Capital for Doing Ministry* (Berea OH: Pilgrim, 2001).

20. Dean R. Hoge and Jacqueline E. Wenger, *Pastors in Transition: Why Clergy Leave Local Church Ministry* (Grand Rapids MI: William B. Eerdmans, 2005) 81.

21. Though not an ordained minister, my wife is a Christian leader still. She has helped me continue to be gracious without being timid about ethical and moral commitments birthed from our identity in Christ. What we have endured as a married couple, we have endured together, as a team. Our journey has not been one of relative ease, so I am grateful to have her beside me "for better or for worse, for richer or for poorer, in sickness and in health, to love and to cherish . . . ."

22. This is a phrase that Lovett H. Weems of Wesley Theological Seminary often mentioned in our 2012–13 Lewis Fellow meetings as he led our discussions.

23. A helpful story of burnout comes from Wayne Cordeiro, *Leading on Empty: Refilling Your Tank and Renewing Your Passion* (Minneapolis: Bethany, 2009).

24. This phrasing comes from two elders in my community—Andrew and Alana Goodwin—whose personal model is to "never let your actions turn your words into hypocrisy."

25. Paul Tournier, *Secrets* (Richmond: John Knox, 1969) 26.

26. John Piper, *Let the Nations Be Glad!: The Supremacy of God in Missions* (Ada MI: Baker Academic, 2010) 50.

27. Names of people and places have been changed to preserve confidentiality.

28. See Matthew 5:11.

29. See 2 Corinthians 12:9.

30. Brian Miller, "Recanting the Baptist Faith and Message," *Associated Baptist Press*, 18 February 2013, www.abpnews.com.

31. Ibid.

32. James Baldwin, *The Fire Next Time* (New York: Vintage, 1995) 8.

33. Bryan T. Calvin, "Resisting a Segregated Church," *Relevant Magazine Online*, 2 March 2012, http://www.relevantmagazine.com/god/church/blog/28480-resisting-a-segregated-church.

34. Charlotte Elliott, "Just as I Am" 1835; David Alkman, *Billy Graham: His Life and Influence* (Nashville: Thomas Nelson, 2007) 138. By 1953 Graham began to call for racial unity and would later only agree to speak to integrated audiences.

35. Imaeyen Ibanga, "Two Nations Under God: Segregated Churches the Norm," *ABC News*, 10 September 2008, http://abcnews.go.com/Politics/5050/story?id=6015620&page=1.

36. Malcolm X, "Black Man's History" *Collected Speeches, Debates & Interviews* (1960–1965), 12 December 1962.

37. Robert Lowry, "Nothing but the Blood," 1876. The *United Methodist Hymnal* has changed the language from "white as snow" to "bright as snow" (Isaiah 1:18).

38. Frederick Douglass, *Narrative of Frederick Douglass* (New Haven: Yale, 2001) 81.

39. Frederick Douglass, "The Church and Prejudice," http://www.frederickdouglass.org/speeches/.

40. James Baldwin, *Go Tell It on the Mountain* (New York: Dell, 1985), 203–204.

41. Alon Harish, "Mississippi Church Refuses to Marry Black Couple," *ABC World News*, 28 July 2012, http://abcnews.go.com/US/mississippi-church-rejects-black-wedding/story?id=16878536#.Uay-TusvobY.

42. Marriage takes two, of course, as do most other forms of relationship. I cannot speak for my ex-wife nor should I. These are merely my impressions. I am learning to take responsibility for my actions in the downfall of our marriage, which is tough when our culture usually prefers the language of blame.

43. Thanks to Martin Luther, who stated long ago, "*Simul justus et peccator,*" that is, "Simultaneously righteous and a sinner." I choose to believe that once we followers of Christ embrace that idea, we may finally taste the fragile beauty of being church.

44. I wonder how social media like Facebook reinforces the *myth of fine*. With every cute picture, update, or post, don't we perpetuate the notion

that "my life is just super, couldn't be better" when the truth is usually much different?

45. John 3:19—"This is the verdict: Light has come into the world, but people loved darkness instead of light because their deeds were evil." It's awfully hard to be authentic if we prefer darkness to light.

46. Stanley Hauerwas, *A Community of Character: Toward a Constructive Christian Social Ethic* (Notre Dame IN: University of Notre Dame, 1981) 33.

47. A century ago, Rev. Charles Jefferson spoke specifically about the give-and-take within the task of preaching. "Preaching is a *reciprocal* business. It is a matter of giving and taking, and the taking is no less important than the giving. A sermon is a joint product, the creation of the preacher and the people. The prosperity of the sermon depends both on the tongue to speak and the ear that hears" (*The Building of the Church* [New York: Macmillan, 1913] 125). See Jefferson's work for what, I believe, is the single most passionate and inspirational series of sermons on a healthy ecclesiology.

48. Luce Irigaray, *Marine Lover of Friedrich Nietzsche*, trans. Gillian Gill (New York: Columbia UP, 1991) 37.

49. Robert Lowry, 1864.

50. The next day over breakfast, I noticed the bishop's name on the front page of the *New York Times* because of the meeting he was in—and left—to talk with me. I later wrote a book on leadership and dedicated it to him.

51. In Barbara E. Taylor and Malcolm L. Warford, eds., *Good Stewardship: A Handbook for Seminary Trustees* (Washington, DC: Association of Governing Boards of Colleges and Universities, 1991) 39.

52. The Reverend Paul Ashby writing on Paul's Epistles in "The Visitor," of Fellowship Congregational (UCC) Church, 2008.

53. H. Richard Niebuhr, *The Purpose of the Church and Its Ministry: Reflections on the Aims of Theological Education* (New York: Harper and Row, Publishers, 1956) 64.

54. LGBT = Lesbian, Gay, Bisexual, Transgender.

55. Karl Barth, *The Humanity of God* (Louisville KY: John Knox, 1960) 95.

Other available titles from

#Connect
Reaching Youth Across the Digital Divide
Brian Foreman

Reaching our youth across the digital divide is a struggle for parents, ministers, and other adults who work with Generation Z—today's teenagers. *#Connect* leads readers into the technological landscape, encourages conversations with teenagers, and reminds us all to be the presence of Christ in every facet of our lives. *978-1-57312-693-9 120 pages/pb* **$13.00**

Beginnings
A Reverend and a Rabbi Talk About the Stories of Genesis
Michael Smith and Rami Shapiro

Editor Aaron Herschel Shapiro declares that stories "must be retold—not just repeated, but reinvented, reimagined, and reexperienced" to remain vital in the world. Mike and Rami continue their conversations from the *Mount and Mountain* books, exploring the places where their traditions intersect and diverge, listening to each other as they respond to the stories of Genesis. *978-1-57312-772-1 202 pages/pb* **$18.00**

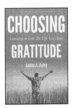

Choosing Gratitude
Learning to Love the Life You Have
James A. Autry

Autry reminds us that gratitude is a choice, a spiritual—not social—process. He suggests that if we cultivate gratitude as a way of being, we may not change the world and its ills, but we can change our response to the world. If we fill our lives with moments of gratitude, we will indeed love the life we have. *978-1-57312-614-4 144 pages/pb* **$15.00**

Choosing Gratitude 365 Days a Year
Your Daily Guide to Grateful Living
James A. Autry and Sally J. Pederson

Filled with quotes, poems, and the inspired voices of both Pederson and Autry, in a society consumed by fears of not having "enough"—money, possessions, security, and so on—this book suggests that if we cultivate gratitude as a way of being, we may not change the world and its ills, but we can change our response to the world. *978-1-57312-689-2 210 pages/pb* **$18.00**

Crossroads in Christian Growth
W. Loyd Allen

Authentic Christian life presents spiritual crises and we struggle to find a hero walking with God at a crossroads. With wisdom and sincerity, W. Loyd Allen presents Jesus as our example and these crises as stages in the journey of growth we each take toward maturity in Christ. *978-1-57312-753-0 164 pages/pb* **$15.00**

A Divine Duet
Ministry and Motherhood
Alicia Davis Porterfield, ed.

Each essay in this inspiring collection is as different as the mother-minister who wrote it, from theologians to chaplains, inner-city ministers to rural-poverty ministers, youth pastors to preachers, mothers who have adopted, birthed, and done both. *978-1-57312-676-2 146 pages/pb* **$16.00**

The Exile and Beyond (All the Bible series)
Wayne Ballard

The Exile and Beyond brings to life the sacred literature of Israel and Judah that comprises the exilic and postexilic communities of faith. It covers Ezekiel, Isaiah, Haggai, Zechariah, Malachi, 1 & 2 Chronicles, Ezra, Nehemiah, Joel, Jonah, Song of Songs, Esther, and Daniel. *978-1-57312-759-2 196 pages/pb* **$16.00**

Ezekiel (Smyth & Helwys Annual Bible Study series)
God's Presence in Performance
William D. Shiell

Through a four-session Bible study for individuals and groups, Shiell interprets the book of Ezekiel as a four-act drama to be told to those living out their faith in a strange, new place. Shiell encourages congregations to listen to God's call, accept where God has planted them, surrender the shame of their past, receive a new heart from God, and allow God to breathe new life into them. *Teaching Guide 978-1-57312-755-4 192 pages/pb* **$14.00**
Study Guide 978-1-57312-756-1 126 pages/pb **$6.00**

Fierce Love
Desperate Measures for Desperate Times
Jeanie Miley

Fierce Love is about learning to see yourself and know yourself as a conduit of love, operating from a full heart instead of trying to find someone to whom you can hook up your emotional hose and fill up your empty heart. *978-1-57312-810-0 276 pages/pb* **$18.00**

Five Hundred Miles
Reflections on Calling and Pilgrimage
Lauren Brewer Bass

Spain's Camino de Santiago, the Way of St. James, has been a cherished pilgrimage path for centuries, visited by countless people searching for healing, solace, purpose, and hope. These stories from her five-hundred-mile-walk is Lauren Brewer Bass's honest look at the often winding, always surprising journey of a calling. *978-1-57312-812-4 142 pages/pb* **$16.00**

Galatians (Smyth & Helwys Bible Commentary)
Marion L. Soards and Darrell J. Pursiful

In Galatians, Paul endeavored to prevent the Gentile converts from embracing a version of the gospel that insisted on their observance of a form of the Mosaic Law. He saw with a unique clarity that such a message reduced the crucified Christ to being a mere agent of the Law. For Paul, the gospel of Jesus Christ alone, and him crucified, had no place in it for the claim that Law-observance was necessary for believers to experience the power of God's grace. *978-1-57312-771-4 384 pages/hc* **$55.00**

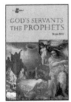

God's Servants the Prophets
Bryan Bibb

God's Servants, the Prophets covers the Israelite and Judean prophetic literature from the preexilic period. It includes Amos, Hosea, Isaiah, Micah, Zephaniah, Nahum, Habakkuk, Jeremiah, and Obadiah. *978-1-57312-758-5 208 pages/pb* **$16.00**

Hermeneutics of Hymnody
A Comprehensive and Integrated Approach to Understanding Hymns
Scotty Gray

Scotty Gray's *Hermeneutics of Hymnody* is a comprehensive and integrated approach to understanding hymns. It is unique in its holistic and interrelated exploration of seven of the broad facets of this most basic forms of Christian literature. A chapter is devoted to each and relates that facet to all of the others. *978-157312-767-7 432 pages/pb* **$28.00**

If Jesus Isn't the Answer . . . He Sure Asks the Right Questions!
J. Daniel Day

Taking eleven of Jesus' questions as its core, Day invites readers into their own conversation with Jesus. Equal parts testimony, theological instruction, pastoral counseling, and autobiography, the book is ultimately an invitation to honest Christian discipleship. *978-1-57312-797-4 148 pages/pb* **$16.00**

I'm Trying to Lead . . . Is Anybody Following?
The Challenge of Congregational Leadership in the Postmodern World
Charles B. Bugg

Bugg provides us with a view of leadership that has theological integrity, honors the diversity of church members, and reinforces the brave hearts of church leaders who offer vision and take risks in the service of Christ and the church.
978-1-57312-731-8 *136 pages/pb* **$13.00**

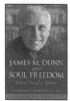

James M. Dunn and Soul Freedom
Aaron Douglas Weaver

James Milton Dunn, over the last fifty years, has been the most aggressive Baptist proponent for religious liberty in the US. Soul freedom—voluntary, uncoerced faith and an unfettered individual conscience before God—is the basis of his understanding of church-state separation and the historic Baptist basis of religious liberty.
978-1-57312-590-1 *224 pages/pb* **$18.00**

The Jesus Tribe
Following Christ in the Land of the Empire
Ronnie McBrayer

The Jesus Tribe fleshes out the implications, possibilities, contradictions, and complexities of what it means to live within the Jesus Tribe and in the shadow of the American Empire.
978-1-57312-592-5 *208 pages/pb* **$17.00**

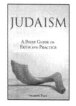

Judaism
A Brief Guide to Faith and Practice
Sharon Pace

Sharon Pace's newest book is a sensitive and comprehensive introduction to Judaism. How does belief in the One God and a universal morality shape the way in which Jews see the world? How does one find meaning in life and the courage to endure suffering? How does one mark joy and forge community ties?
978-1-57312-644-1 *144 pages/pb* **$16.00**

Looking Around for God
The Strangely Reverent Observations of an Unconventional Christian
James A. Autry

Looking Around for God, Autry's tenth book, is in many ways his most personal. In it he considers his unique life of faith and belief in God. Autry is a former Fortune 500 executive, author, poet, and consultant whose work has had a significant influence on leadership thinking.
978-157312-484-3 *144 pages/pb* **$16.00**

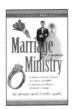

Marriage Ministry: A Guidebook
Bo Prosser and Charles Qualls

This book is equally helpful for ministers, for nearly/newlywed couples, and for thousands of couples across our land looking for fresh air in their marriages. *1-57312-432-X 160 pages/pb* **$16.00**

Meeting Jesus Today
For the Cautious, the Curious, and the Committed

Jeanie Miley

Meeting Jesus Today, ideal for both individual study and small groups, is intended to be used as a workbook. It is designed to move readers from studying the Scriptures and ideas within the chapters to recording their journey with the Living Christ.

978-1-57312-677-9 320 pages/pb **$19.00**

The Ministry Life
101 Tips for Ministers' Spouses

John and Anne Killinger

While no pastor does his or her work alone, roles for a spouse or partner are much more flexible and fluid now than they once were. Spouses who want to support their minister-mates' vocation may wonder where to begin. Whatever your talents may be, the Killingers have identified a way to put those gifts to work. *978-1-57312-769-1 252 pages/pb* **$19.00**

The Ministry Life
101 Tips for New Ministers

John Killinger

Sharing years of wisdom from more than fifty years in ministry and teaching, *The Ministry Life: 101 Tips for New Ministers* by John Killinger is filled with practical advice and wisdom for a minister's day-to-day tasks as well as advice on intellectual and spiritual habits to keep ministers of any age healthy and fulfilled. *978-1-57312-662-5 244 pages/pb* **$19.00**

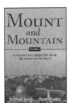

Mount and Mountain
Vol. 2: A Reverend and a Rabbi Talk About the Sermon on the Mount

Rami Shapiro and Michael Smith

This book, focused on the Sermon on the Mount, represents the second half of Mike and Rami's dialogue. In it, Mike and Rami explore the text of Jesus' sermon cooperatively, contributing perspectives drawn from their lives and religious traditions and seeking moments of illumination. *978-1-57312-654-0 254 pages/pb* **$19.00**

Of Mice and Ministers
Musings and Conversations About Life, Death, Grace, and Everything
Bert Montgomery

With stories about pains, joys, and everyday life, *Of Mice and Ministers* finds Jesus in some unlikely places and challenges us to do the same. From tattooed women ministers to saying the "N"-word to the brotherly kiss, Bert Montgomery takes seriously the lesson from Psalm 139—where can one go that God is not already there? *978-1-57312-733-2 154 pages/pb* **$14.00**

Place Value
The Journey to Where You Are
Katie Sciba

Does a place have value? Can a place change us? Is it possible for God to use the place you are in to form you? From Victoria, Texas to Indonesia, Belize, Australia, and beyond, Katie Sciba's wanderlust serves as a framework to understand your own places of deep emotion and how God may have been weaving redemption around you all along.

978-157312-829-2 138 pages/pb **$15.00**

Preacher Breath
Sermon & Essays
Kyndall Rae Rothaus

"*Preacher Breath* is a worthy guide, leading the reader room by room with wisdom, depth, and a spiritual maturity far beyond her years, so that the preaching house becomes a holy, joyful home. . . . This book is soul kindle for a preacher's heart." —Danielle Shroyer
Pastor, Author of *The Boundary-Breaking God*
978-1-57312-734-9 208 pages/pb **$16.00**

Quiet Faith
An Introvert's Guide to Spiritual Survival
Judson Edwards

In eight finely crafted chapters, Edwards looks at key issues like evangelism, interpreting the Bible, dealing with doubt, and surviving the church from the perspective of a confirmed, but sometimes reluctant, introvert. In the process, he offers some provocative insights that introverts will find helpful and reassuring. *978-1-57312-681-6 144 pages/pb* **$15.00**

Reading Deuteronomy
(Reading the Old Testament series)
A Literary and Theological Commentary

Stephen L. Cook

A lost treasure for large segments of today's world, the book of Deuteronomy stirs deep longing for God and moves readers to a place of intimacy with divine otherness, holism, and will for person-centered community. The consistently theological interpretation reveals the centrality of this book for faith. 978-1-57312-757-8 *286 pages/pb* **$22.00**

Reflective Faith
A Theological Toolbox for Women

Susan M. Shaw

In *Reflective Faith*, Susan Shaw offers a set of tools to explore difficult issues of biblical interpretation, theology, church history, and ethics—especially as they relate to women. Reflective faith invites intellectual struggle and embraces the unknown; it is a way of discipleship, a way to love God with your mind, as well as your heart, your soul, and your strength. 978-1-57312-719-6 *292 pages/pb* **$24.00**
Workbook 978-1-57312-754-7 *164 pages/pb* **$12.00**

Sessions with Psalms (Sessions Bible Studies series)
Prayers for All Seasons

Eric and Alicia D. Porterfield

Useful to seminar leaders during preparation and group discussion, as well as in individual Bible study, *Sessions with Psalms* is a ten-session study designed to explore what it looks like for the words of the psalms to become the words of our prayers. Each session is followed by a thought-provoking page of questions. 978-1-57312-768-4 *136 pages/pb* **$14.00**

Sessions with Revelation
(Sessions Bible Studies series)
The Final Days of Evil

David Sapp

David Sapp's careful guide through Revelation demonstrates that it is a letter of hope for believers; it is less about the last days of history than it is about the last days of evil. Without eliminating its mystery, Sapp unlocks Revelation's central truths so that its relevance becomes clear.
978-1-57312-706-6 *166 pages/pb* **$14.00**

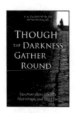

Though the Darkness Gather Round
Devotions about Infertility, Miscarriage, and Infant Loss
Mary Elizabeth Hill Hanchey and Erin McClain, eds.

Much courage is required to weather the long grief of infertility and the sudden grief of miscarriage and infant loss. This collection of devotions by men and women, ministers, chaplains, and lay leaders who can speak of such sorrow, is a much-needed resource and precious gift for families on this journey and the faith communities that walk beside them.

978-1-57312-811-7 180 pages/pb **$19.00**

Time for Supper
Invitations to Christ's Table
Brett Younger

Some scholars suggest that every meal in literature is a communion scene. Could every meal in the Bible be a communion text? Could every passage be an invitation to God's grace? These meditations on the Lord's Supper help us listen to the myriad of ways God invites us to gratefully, reverently, and joyfully share the cup of Christ. *978-1-57312-720-2 246 pages/pb* **$18.00**

A Time to Laugh
Humor in the Bible
Mark E. Biddle

With characteristic liveliness, Mark E. Biddle explores the ways humor was intentionally incorporated into Scripture. Drawing on Biddle's command of Hebrew language and cultural subtleties, *A Time to Laugh* guides the reader through the stories of six biblical characters who did rather unexpected things. *978-1-57312-683-0 164 pages/pb* **$14.00**

A True Hope
Jedi Perils and the Way of Jesus
Joshua Hays

Star Wars offers an accessible starting point for considering substantive issues of faith, philosophy, and ethics. In *A True Hope*, Joshua Hays explores some of these challenging ideas through the sayings of the Jedi Masters, examining the ways the worldview of the Jedi is at odds with that of the Bible. *978-1-57312-770-7 186 pages/pb* **$18.00**

Word of God Across the Ages
Using Christian History in Preaching

Bill J. Leonard

In this third, enlarged edition, Bill J. Leonard returns to the roots of the Christian story to find in the lives of our faithful forebears examples of the potent presence of the gospel. Through these stories, those who preach today will be challenged and inspired as they pursue the divine Word in human history through the ages.   *978-1-57312-828-5 174 pages/pb* **$19.00**

The World Is Waiting for You
Celebrating the 50th Ordination Anniversary of Addie Davis

Pamela R. Durso & LeAnn Gunter Johns, eds.

Hope for the church and the world is alive and well in the words of these gifted women. Keen insight, delightful observations, profound courage, and a gift for communicating the good news are woven throughout these sermons. The Spirit so evident in Addie's calling clearly continues in her legacy.   *978-1-57312-732-5 224 pages/pb* **$18.00**

William J. Reynolds
Church Musician

David W. Music

William J. Reynolds is renowned among Baptist musicians, music ministers, song leaders, and hymnody students. In eminently readable style, David W. Music's comprehensive biography describes Reynolds's family and educational background, his career as a minister of music, denominational leader, and seminary professor.   *978-1-57312-690-8 358 pages/pb* **$23.00**

With Us in the Wilderness
Finding God's Story in Our Lives

Laura A. Barclay

What stories compose your spiritual biography? In *With Us in the Wilderness*, Laura Barclay shares her own stories of the intersection of the divine and the everyday, guiding readers toward identifying and embracing God's presence in their own narratives.

978-1-57312-721-9 120 pages/pb **$13.00**

26993231R00112

Made in the USA
Middletown, DE
09 December 2015